Ballet and Modern Dance

Ballet and

Modern Dance

Craig Dodd

PHAIDON

Acknowledgments

During the compiling of this book, which contains well over 200 photographs, I have been greatly helped by the generosity of many friends in the dance world.

In particular I am grateful to Mary Clarke and Jocelyn Adams of *The Dancing Times* for generously making available their extensive photographic collection. They produced a wealth of historic material as well as many present-day photographs.

Detailed photographic acknowledgments appear at the end of the book, but I am particularly indebted to Mike Davis and Jesse Davis for many photographs of recent performances, as well as such invaluable material as the photograph of the young Nureyev rehearsing in Leningrad.

Anthony Crickmay produced the photograph of Nureyev as the Golden Slave which captures the spirit of the role, as well as the breathtaking view of him in a modern ballet. I am also grateful to Peggy Leder for allowing me to use the series of photographs of Lynn Seymour which convey perfectly the quality of Isadora Duncan's dancing.

David Palmer made available at short notice photographs of the National Ballet of Canada and the Australian Ballet, which saved me much time, as did the Novosti Press Agency with its complete coverage of Soviet Ballet.

I have used photographs of American dance from the excellent series of programs produced by the Public Broadcasting Corporation, channel WNET–13, with the sponsorship of the Exxon Corporation, as well as those by the great photographer Martha Swope.

Some material comes from my own collection and many photographs were contributed by dancers. I have attempted to attribute these correctly and if I have made any errors I would be pleased to hear from the photographers concerned and will correct the entry in future editions.

Craig Dodd

Phaidon Press Limited,
Littlegate House, St Ebbe's Street, Oxford
First published in 1980
© Basinghall Books Limited, 1980
Published in the USA by E.P. Dutton, New York

DESIGNED AND PICTURE-EDITED BY CRAIG DODD

ISBN 0 7148 2050 4
Printed in Hong Kong
by South China Printing Co.

Half-title page: Marylin Rowe and John Meehan of the Australian Ballet in John Cranko's Onegin.

Previous pages: Peter Schaufuss in a spectacular leap from Le Corsaire.

Opposite: Robert Powell in Martha Graham's Clytemnestra.

Contents

Court Dance to Classical Ballet

The Growth of Ballet and Modern Dance

Ballet and Modern Dance Today

Court Dance
to Classical Ballet

Karen Kain as Odile, the Black Swan.

From Court to Theater

Dancing entertainments were common in the late fifteenth and sixteenth centuries. They were conceived on a grand scale for the pleasure of princes or on a smaller scale as travelling shows for the common people. In both cases dancing was part of a general performance which would include a mixture of acrobatics, mime, speech and song.

Following the most famous example of a court entertainment at the end of the fourteenth century, that given to celebrate the marriage of the Duke of Milan to Isabella of Aragon, Italian princes vied with each other in the splendor of their banquets. These court entertainments had a political significance. They not only showed off the magnificence of the court, but were written and conceived as subtle propaganda. A visiting dignitary about to start negotiations of state could be flattered by some allusion to his talents, be given some hint as to his host's intentions or quite simply be threatened by a show of strength.

These entertainments were usually peopled by allegorical figures and employed acrobats and mechanical effects. Elaborately decorated tableaux would be drawn on in gilded carriages like floats in a carnival today. If presented during a banquet, each *entrée* would be accompanied by some suitably enhancing theme; the fish course for instance, might be accompanied by a tableau with a watery motif, including Neptune and underwater creatures.

Above: The entry of the Satyrs in the Ballet Comique de la Reine, *1581.*

Below: Louis XIV as the Sun in La Nuit, *1653.*

Travelling ballet masters, who moved from court to court across Europe, arranged these pageants. Sometimes they used professional performers, sometimes the monarch and his court took part. They also arranged ballets for the king's horses and their meticulously arranged maneuvers have given us the art of dressage (seen at its peak in the Spanish Riding School in Vienna). From these derive some ballet terms, for instance *manège*, when a dancer does a series of steps circling the stage.

Catherine de Medici took the art of court entertainment with her to France when she married King Henry II and it was here that it was refined to a peak of perfection. Her motives were still as much political as artistic and she used the *ballet de cour* to divert her sons (three of whom became kings of France – Francis II, Charles IX and Henry III) while she wielded the actual power. Catherine employed the services of a famous violinist, Balthasar de Beaujoyeulx, as her ballet master and it was he who was responsible for her greatest achievement, the *Ballet Comique de la Reine*. This was created at Catherine's command to celebrate the wedding of the Duc de Joyeuse to Margaret of Lorraine in 1581 and it was fully documented in an elaborate book the following year. This epic piece, which lasted over five and a half hours, did not, it is reported, weary or displease the audience.

It is from this point that the history of ballet is commonly said to have begun. Court ladies took part in it, which was in itself unusual, as dancing had hitherto been limited to men. Even in popular performances the women's roles had, as in Shakespearean drama, been taken by men. The steps this first recorded *corps de ballet* took amounted to little more than elaborate walking. The great invention lay in the overall plan and the complicated floor patterns. Intricate steps, turns and jumps did not appear for almost a century. In any case such steps would not have been possible because the ladies wore, as they continued to wear right into the eighteenth century, cumbersome, hooped court dress. Men wore tights as part of everyday dress and thus had greater freedom to show off a well-turned leg, which soon became a necessity in the dance, and a finely pointed foot.

The next most important, and well recorded, *ballet de cour* took place during the reign of Louis XIV. In it he personified (among other roles) the Sun King, an image which became closely associated with him and his reign. Louis is perhaps the most important figure in the transition of dance from court entertainment to professional occupation. His own love of dancing from an early age gave it respectability, and his courtiers, politicians and even one particularly talented Field Marshal devoted much of their energy to it, achieving great proficiency. It was a period when Molière devised subjects and Lully and Beauchamps wrote music. Molière's plays invariably included dance scenes and from him the ballet acquired an occasional touch of comedy to lighten the edifying diet of exalted allegory.

Louis performed the first formal act to establish ballet as a professional theatrical art by creating the Royal Academy of the Dance and the associated Royal Academy of Music in 1661. A school of dance was added in 1671 and from this reorganization the Paris Opéra of today has grown. Louis gave dance one more impulse by giving up dancing, after appearing in the ballet *Flore* in 1669. He was by then too fat. Naturally the court had to follow suit, leaving the field open for the professional dancer.

By the end of the seventeenth century and in the early years of the eighteenth, we have all the foundations of ballet as we know it today. Ballet masters had begun to codify teaching, the five positions of the feet had been recorded (not invented) by Beauchamps, there had been attempts at dance notation, costume had begun to change to allow more intricate footwork and we see the natural emergence of the ballerina to a position of dominance.

Up to this time the technique of the ballet was firmly earth-bound. Free-flowing movement, jumps and lifts were not possible, let alone socially acceptable, in the court. If an effect of lightness or flight was needed it had to be achieved by complicated machinery. The only variations of effect were achieved through changing floor patterns or different tempi. It is also worth noting that even now 'ballet' continued to be a combination of dancing, music and singing, with the singing often taking precedence. The performers were also always masked.

Below: Marie de Camargo, with musicians watching her dangerously obvious ankles, in the painting by Lancret.

Female dancers did not appear on the stage until 1681. In the early performances they were court ladies, but later the Academy of Music supplied four ballerinas. They were led by Mademoiselle Lafontaine, who thus became the first prima ballerina! However, Marie de Camargo was the first true ballerina to establish herself and to progress the art of ballet. She was famous for the speed and neatness of her footwork and is credited with introducing the *entrechat quatre*, as well as some *jetés*. To show off her footwork she shortened her skirt just a few inches, but this was not to prove completely acceptable for nearly half a century.

Her great contemporary Marie Sallé met with similar problems and left the Opéra to work in London where standards were not so strict. She was allowed to dance in the ballet *Pygmalion* at Covent Garden wearing only classical draperies, but it was nearly fifteen years before the same role could be danced in Paris, similarly dressed. Until then the hooped skirt was rigidly adhered to.

By 1760 ballet masters were beginning to question these restrictions on their art, restrictions which were an unwanted hangover from the days when the ballet was part of the court with its rigid protocol. Greatest of these ballet masters was Jean Georges Noverre, born in 1727. He was obliged to leave France to further his cause and was invited to London, by David Garrick, to work at Drury Lane. He later settled in Stuttgart where he directed a company of over a hundred dancers for the Duke of Wurtenburg.

Left: A scene from Il Pastor Fido, *one of the carefully researched productions at the Swedish Court Theater at Drottningholm.*

Noverre, in his *Letters*, first proposed ideas which were to become central to the development of ballet as a serious art form. He believed that ballet should be a means of expressing a dramatic idea through the perfect combination of dancing, drama and character. Speech, either declaimed or sung, was to be discarded, as were the restricting wigs, masks and cumbersome costumes. In Stuttgart he worked out his ideas with his students, including the great dancer Vestris and the choreographer Dauberval. Vestris, the God of the Dance, was the greatest male dancer of the age. He had a noble style and excelled at jumps and the newly invented *pirouettes*, first performed by Anne Heinel.

Vestris' son Auguste, who inherited the title of 'God of the Dance' from his father, held the post of *premier danseur* at the Opéra for thirty-six years. He is reported as having had an excellent technique with great elevation and the ability to execute *entrechats* and *pirouettes*. He fitted equally well into every type of ballet and there was never any stress in his dancing. Such all-round brilliance certainly merited his exalted title. It was Dauberval, however, who was able to put Noverre's teaching to most immediate use and he also passed on the ideas to Salvatore Vigano, who brought them to full realization.

After working with Dauberval, Vigano established himself in Milan, having inherited a fortune from an admirer. Here he gave up dancing and spent all his time on choreography. He had the signal honor of creating the only ballet Beethoven wrote, *The Creatures of Prometheus*.

Yet another of Dauberval's pupils was Carlo Blasis, who returned to Italy to work with Vigano. He devoted most of his energies to teaching and in 1820 published his first treatise. When he finally stopped dancing, following an accident in 1837, he took over the school at La Scala. He also found time to create over 70 ballets, but it was his contribution to teaching which proved invaluable to the classic tradition in Russia.

Dauberval himself put into practice, perhaps more successfully than his master, most of Noverre's principles. In his ballet *La Fille Mal Gardée*, created in Bordeaux in 1789, he put real people on the stage for the first time. It was a complete story involving farmers, lovers, lawyers and harvesters. The story was carried forward by integrated dance and mime. Sadly, only the title and inspiration of this ballet remain. For the roots of the popular versions we see today, we must look to the revival in Paris in 1828 when the great Romantic Age was emerging and to the revivals of 1864 and 1884 in Russia when ballet had moved into its classical period.

Below: Drawings of Salvatore Vigano and his wife, Maria Medina, by Schadow. Maria wore flesh-coloured tights under flowing crêpe, a daring innovation at that time.

La Fille Mal Gardée

Top right: Brenda Last and Desmond Kelly in Frederick Ashton's La Fille Mal Gardée.

Bottom right: Karen Kain and Frank Augustyn of the National Ballet of Canada as Lise and Colas, with David Roxander as Alain.

La Fille Mal Gardée is one of the most charming and most popular ballets in the current repertoire. In name and theme it is also one of the oldest. *The Whims of Cupid*, created by Galeotti just three years earlier in Copenhagen, has the firmest claim to be the oldest ballet extant as it has had a history of continuous revival by the Royal Danish Ballet. It would, however, be fair to assume that as dance technique progressed, the steps we now see are somewhat more complicated than those created by Galeotti.

Jean Dauberval was a student of the great Noverre and made his debut at the Paris Opéra in 1761, becoming a principal dancer nine years later. After his retirement from the post of assistant ballet master at the Opéra he took over the direction of the ballet in Bordeaux. It was here, in 1789, that he created *La Fille Mal Gardée* with his wife taking the part of Lise. Two years later it was presented in London where it first acquired the title by which it is now known, a title which appears to defy satisfactory translation into English. It has been presented as *Vain Precautions* and *Naughty Lisette*, neither of which quite captures the charm of the story!

All trace of this production has been lost except for the knowledge that the music was a *pot-pouri* of popular tunes of the day. A ballet of this title and story was produced in Paris in 1828 with a new score by Hérold, to which a *pas de deux* with music by Donizetti was added when Fanny Elssler danced it in 1837. Frederick Ashton's charming version for the Royal Ballet uses mostly the Hérold music, cleverly arranged by John Lanchberry. It also includes the famous mime scene used by Virginia Zucchi from the revival by Petipa and Ivanov in 1885. That revival used yet another score, from the 1864 production in Berlin written by Hertel. This score is still used in Russia and America.

The ballet has rarely been out of the repertoire. Anna Pavlova performed a one-act version, taking it on tour to America. Her former partner, Mikhail Mordkin, produced the first American version in 1937, in which Lucia Chase danced Lise for the New York premiere. American Ballet Theater, the company she went on to direct for many years, produced their version (a reworking of the Mordkin production by Bronislav Nijinska, Nijinsky's sister) just two years later for their own first season.

From a brief glimpse of a charming print in a shop window, Dauberval created the story of Lise, her widowed mother, Colas the younger farmer she loves and Alain whom her mother wishes her to marry. Some 200 years later the freshness of that inspiration is still apparent.

Right: Jacques Gorrissen of the National Ballet of Canada as the Widow Simone.

The Romantic Age

After nearly two centuries of being firmly earth-bound, ballet finally took off, both literally and aesthetically, during the first part of the nineteenth century. Technique had progressed, with the principle of the full turn-out of the legs established. Costume was freer, not just as a result of Noverre's teaching, but also through a breaking down of the old regime by the French Revolution.

Ballet had no sooner established itself firmly in the theater with principles of artistic integrity and produced one lasting ballet, *La Fille Mal Gardée*, as a testimony to this advance, when there came an intense reaction. Swept along by a general wave of artistic feeling, ballet embarked on a short-lived but remarkably creative period, a period which left a permanent legacy.

If Noverre's principles were temporarily cast aside and the work of his pupils in France forgotten for some time, one fact of real importance emerged. Ballet had been established as a serious, independent art form. As such it was totally involved in the romantic revolution in all the arts, accepted not only as an equal, but expanding its possibilities in several directions. The image of the romantic ballerina, captured in many fine prints, became an image of the movement.

Left: Alicia Markova, who captured completely the charm, style and spirit of the Romantic Age.

Top right: Lucille Grahn, the Danish ballerina who created the Sylphide in Bournonville's production.

Top Left: A period engraving of Marie Taglioni which makes her look more robust than the image she created on the stage.

Above: The fiery Fanny Elssler who created the Cachucha, *which was then danced by other ballerinas such as Grahn.*

The world of the imagination became paramount. The affairs of ordinary folk, the farmers of *La Fille Mal Gardée*, were of no interest compared to the agonies of the poet. The realistic farmyard gave way to the haunted glen. The eternal pursuit of the muse, the agonies of creation and the search for artistic perfection became central to artists, writers and musicians. Their interest was in the supernatural, the unattainable.

The ballets of this period, particularly *La Sylphide* and *Giselle*, were both part and result of the revolution, alongside the paintings of Delacroix, the music of Berlioz, the literature of Victor Hugo and E.T.A. Hoffman, whose story *The Nutcracker and the Mouse-king* reappeared later in the century. Reality was out; fantasy was the order of the day. The anguish and ordeals of the poet in *Symphonie Fantastique* found perfect expression through the ballet and, perhaps most importantly, through the romantic ballerina.

Marie Taglioni was the pale, ethereal, overworked daughter of the choreographer Filipo Taglioni. She was born in Stockholm in 1804 and was trained in Paris while her father worked throughout Europe. He did not approve of her training and set her a rigorous regime designed with one aim in mind: to make her the greatest dancer in Europe.

Taglioni finally made her Paris debut in 1827 and was immediately noted for her aerial quality and floating grace while on point, a technique which was already in use at the beginning of the century. These qualities were exactly those needed to capture the other-worldliness of most of the romantic roles. In 1831, aged 27, she appeared in the indifferent Meyerbeer opera, *Robert the Devil*, as the Abbess leading her ghostly nuns through the haunted cloisters, the first romantic ballet.

Left: Margarethe Schanne, one of the greatest recent performers of the role of the Sylphide, with Henning Kronstam as James.

A central and influential figure in the romantic movement was the critic and poet Theóphile Gautier. Neither a dancer nor a choreographer, he was an important catalyst, in much the same way that Jean Cocteau was with the Diaghilev Ballet later. He had a clear vision of the romantic ideal, an ideal which was summed up for him by the ballerina Carlotta Grisi, the first Giselle. He devised this ballet for her and it was to prove the high point of the romantic era. However, his devotion was not returned and he settled for marrying her sister. It is reported that he died with Carlotta's name on his lips, truly a romantic situation.

Immediately after her success in *Robert the Devil*, Taglioni began work on the new ballet being created for her by her father. This was *La Sylphide*, the first complete romantic ballet. The very name evokes the spirit of the age and sylphs have floated through countless ballets ever since. The costume has become a standard dress with its tight-fitting bodice, leaving the neck and shoulders bare, a bell-shaped tulle skirt reaching half way between knee and ankle, and pink tights and pink satin shoes. These were not the substantially blocked ones used now, but were softer; the ballerina had to rely on darning to strengthen them for point work.

Below: Peter Schaufuss, brought up in the Danish tradition, in a typical Bournonville jump in the second act of La Sylphide.

The production by Filipo Taglioni at the Paris Opéra in 1832 now exists only in reconstructed form, the original having been forgotten during the long decline of the Opéra in the last half of the nineteenth century. The version most commonly seen today is that created by Auguste Bournonville in Copenhagen in 1836. Undoubtedly he used his memories of the Paris production, but he utilized a new score by Lovenskjold and the choreography is unmistakably his own. The ballet has never been out of the repertoire of the Royal Danish Ballet since it was first danced by Lucille Grahn, another of the five great ballerinas of the age.

La Sylphide is set in Scotland, at that time a land sufficiently remote to suggest swirling mists, witches and sylphs. It is quite probable that Bournonville made more of the Scottish folk element than the original since he had a great interest in national dances. He exploited them throughout his career in such ballets as *Far from Denmark* and *The Toreador*, his interest predating the general trend at the time of *Coppelia* and *Don Quixote*. The sylph of the title is a capricious creature who eventually causes the hero, James, to lose his bride and his sanity. He pursues her, but never quite catches her, a clear allusion to the muse-poet relationship.

In Paris, James was danced by Joseph Mazilier, who went on to create *Paquita*.

Taglioni as the Sylph secured a triumph, a fortune and an enormous following across Europe. Sadly she did not find another role of similar stature. The next great role of the romantic era was created by Carlotta Grisi.

Théophile Gautier was inspired to devise *Giselle* by the old German legend of the Wilis, girls who died before their wedding day, as recounted by Heinrich Heine. The music was written in a week by Adolph Adam and the choreography was by Coralli and Perrot. As Grisi was Perrot's mistress at the time and both had excellent relations with Adam, it can safely be assumed that Perrot was at least responsible for most of Grisi's choreography while Coralli created the rest.

Perrot had previously been a dancer at the Opéra and had partnered Taglioni in *Zéphire et Flore* in 1834. However, he had left in disgust at the constant intrigues and, it is reported, in order to be with Grisi. They appeared together with great success in London, Vienna and Munich, mainly in ballets by Perrot. After the success of *Giselle*, Perrot returned to London where he created several successful works including *Esmeralda*.

Following the premiere of *Giselle* at the Opéra in 1841, it was produced in London in 1842, again with Grisi in the title role. Perrot himself danced the role of Albrecht which had been created by Lucien Petipa, the talented dancer brother of Marius Petipa. Four years later saw the American premiere danced, suitably enough, by American dancers. Mary Ann Lee had studied with Coralli in Paris and she was partnered by George Washington Smith.

Above: Mikhail Baryshnikov and Natalia Makarova in the first act of the American Ballet Theater Giselle.

Top left: Elaine MacDonald as Giselle collapses at the end of the mad scene in the first act of the Scottish Ballet Giselle.

Bottom left: Patricia Rianne as Myrtha, Queen of the Wilis, with the Wilis in their unusual dresses in the Scottish Ballet Giselle.

Above: Mikhail Baryshnikov in the more traditional second act of the American Ballet Theater Giselle, *with the Wilis in typical 'romantic' skirts.*

the major ballerinas and a great element of the cult of personality. Perhaps the poets, critics and painters who were the champions of the cause began to identify the ballerinas too closely with their muses. In any case the Director of the Opéra, Dr Veron, had an eye for publicity and was determined to make the Opéra a financial success. It was he who encouraged such overripe operas as *Robert the Devil*, with their lavish ballets. Presumably Dr Veron knew what would bring the patrons in and for once it coincided with the creative thrust of the time.

There was fierce rivalry from the start between Taglioni and Fanny Elssler which certainly helped generate interest in their performances. The two dancers appear to have had little in common, but a closer study of their careers suggests that they may have had more in common than generally thought.

Taglioni, with her ethereal image, was called the first Christian dancer, which suggests a coolness and lack of sex appeal. Fanny Elssler specialized in more colorful and earthy roles, together with character dances such as her famous *Cachucha*, a Spanish dance. The implication is that Taglioni was a greater artist, but from the way Elssler's career expanded until she developed her dramatic talents to become one of the great Giselles, it appears she had a greater intelligence and range. She also did much pioneer touring in America and was the first romantic ballerina to appear there. During 1840 she had great triumphs in places as far apart as New York and New Orleans.

Above: Ekaterina Maximova and Vladimir Tikhonov in the Bolshoi Ballet Giselle.

Right: Alla Sizova and Sergei Vikulov in the Kirov Giselle.

Above: Veronica Tennant as Lise in the first act of the National Ballet of Canada's La Fille Mal Gardée.

Left: Peter Schaufuss in the brilliant solo for Colas on his way to the harvest in La Fille Mal Gardée.

The other ballerinas who dominated the age were the three who joined Taglioni for the famous *Pas de Quatre*: Lucille Grahn, Carlotta Grisi and Fanny Cerrito. Grisi had been the first Giselle, Grahn the Danish Sylphide and Cerrito the first Ondine. Gathering together these four ballerinas was the idea of Benjamin Lumley at Her Majesty's Theatre, London. This was to be the apotheosis of the romantic age. We can only guess about Perrot's choreography, but there have been witty and charming reconstructions by Anton Dolin and Keith Lester. The four ballerinas were also captured in their final tableau in the famous lithograph by Chalon.

Romanticism had burned itself out in less than fifteen years. In France ballet degenerated. Ballerinas and choreographers sought new outlets. Marius Petipa left for St Petersburg in 1847.

The Rise of Russia

Before the arrival of Marius Petipa, Russia had a tradition of dance founded on Peter the Great's aim to 'westernize' his country. During his reign (1672–1725) he introduced dancing along with other social reforms as a civilizing influence. Inevitably that influence was primarily French since during this period France was the center of dance activity and already had a national Academy. Not to be outdone, the Empress Anne founded a Russian Academy of Dance and brought a Frenchman, Landé, to direct it. This was eventually to develop into the Imperial School, allied to the Imperial Theater in St Petersburg. The Austrian ballet master Hilferding was invited to Russia by the beautiful Empress Elizabeth who was fond of dancing. He mounted not only his latest works, but also introduced the first hints of Russian subjects into the court entertainments. Catherine the Great increased dance activity and invited Hilferding's pupil, the Italian Angiolini, to Russia. His great strength was in producing very theatrical works and some of his ideas about dance-drama predate those of Noverre.

Other French dancers began to find Russia a fruitful outlet for their creativity, especially those who had left France for Milan (to work with Carlo Blasis) as a result of the Revolution. These were followed, as the romantic age declined, by dancers and choreographers disillusioned by the sad state of ballet in France. Perhaps the most

Below: Margaret Barbieri as Swanhilda in the new production of Coppelia *by Peter Wright for the Royal Ballet.*

Bottom left: Peter Schaufuss as a surprised Franz in Erik Bruhn's version of Coppelia *danced by the National Ballet of Canada.*

Bottom right: Maria Guerrero as Swanhilda in Alfonso Cata's ingenious production of Coppelia *in Frankfurt.*

influential visitor in the early years of Russian ballet was Charles Didelot, who arrived in 1801. Born in Stockholm, he had studied with Noverre, Dauberval and Vestris, and brought to Russia the best ideas of French teaching. These he combined with a reorganization of the system he found at the St Petersburg School. Marius Petipa was able to build on this solid base and the natural talent he found there.

In France Marius Petipa left behind a world of ballet in decline. The glorious romantic age had burned itself out and sadly no phoenix grew out of the ashes. Instead the cult of the ballerina became supreme – the ballerina as idol and not as dancer. The great ballerinas of the age had left Paris or retired. Musicians and choreographers had no creative urge and ballet became a spectacle for the dilettante. Access to the *foyer de la danse* became more important than the performance. In any case the performance was regarded as a social event for gentlemen to ogle the *corps de ballet*. Most of the principles of Noverre were forgotten and the male dancer was regarded as an unnecessary encumbrance. The audience wished to see either a row of scantily clad girls or each other. It was not for artistic reasons that the role of Franz in *Coppelia* was danced by a girl, usually the prettiest and most voluptuous. It was simply an excuse to see a shapely leg in tights.

This degrading of ballet was particularly sad in the case of *Coppelia* which has proved to be a lasting work full of invention and with an especially glorious score by Leo Delibes. By the time it was created in 1870 the general state of ballet in France was at a particularly low point. It was not until over 60 years later that there were any signs of recovery. The demise of the romantic movement was long since completed but at least one of Noverre's principles had been salvaged.

Above: Margaret Barbieri and David Ashmole in the Royal Ballet Coppelia.

Left: Two scenes from the colorful production of Coppelia *devised by Ulf Gadd for the Gothenburg Ballet.*
Top: Helen Sjostedt, Vilgot Gyllengran and Katerina Wester in the pas de trois *from act one.*
Bottom: The can-can finale is danced by the whole company in costumes and settings by Sven-Erik Goude, who collaborated on this production of a Coppelia *played as boulevard theater of the 1900s.*

Right: Lucette Aldous and Rudolf Nureyev in the Australian Ballet Don Quixote, *produced on stage and film by Nureyev.*

Coppelia is a ballet about real people in real surroundings, in spite of becoming involved with the mysterious Dr Coppelius and his magic dolls. The national dances, such as the Hungarian Czardas, were an innovation, although they had been predated by Bournonville's work in Copenhagen. Very little of St Leon's original choreography remains and we are once again indebted to Marius Petipa for the basis of versions performed regularly today.

Marius Petipa originally went to St Petersburg as a dancer, having been over-shadowed in France by his brother Lucien. Russia was a natural place to expand his talents as the tradition of male dancing had not been allowed to go into decline and would prove one of its greatest strengths in the years to come. By 1862 Petipa was working as ballet master under St Leon, who held the post of chief Ballet Master. He had already had great success with his choreography for *The Pharaoh's Daughter* and when St Leon left for Paris in 1869 to produce *Coppelia*, Petipa took over his post and held it until his retirement in 1903. During this time he choreographed over 60 full-length ballets of which two are the mainstay of the ballet repertory today. This may seem a small proportion, but into *The Sleeping Beauty* and *Swan Lake* he poured all his mastery of choreography, construction and drama.

In Copenhagen Auguste Bournonville started a new tradition. One of his classes is immortalised in the ballet Conservatoire, *seen below with Nilas Martins, son of Peter Martins, as a pupil and Flemming Ryberg as the ballet master. His interest in national dances resulted in ballets such as* Toreador, Napoli *and* Far From Denmark. *Dancers from the Royal Danish Ballet in the early 1920s posed for some of the more famous dances. Opposite, in the top row, there is the Jockey Dance from* From Siberia to Moscow, *and also the Chinese and Indian Dances from* Far From Denmark. *In the bottom row future director of the company, Harald Lander, poses as Gennaro in* Napoli.

34

Right: Malika Sabirova, one of Ulanova's pupils, dances one of the variations in Petipa's Don Quixote *at the Bolshoi.*

Below: Nazhdezska Pavlova, the young star of the Bolshoi Ballet, in an uncharacteristically happy mood as Kitri in Don Quixote.

Left: Ib Andersen, one of the young stars of the Royal Danish Ballet in Bournonville's Toreador.

In the year of his appointment he choreographed *Don Quixote* at the Bolshoi Theater in Moscow. He used the Cervantes story of the Don and his adventures, with an additional plot about two lovers, Kitri and Basilio. The music was by Minkus who was the resident composer at the Bolshoi. He had previously essayed into Spanish territory when he collaborated on the score for *Paquita* which Petipa had revived (the original was by Mazilier in Paris, for Carlotta Grisi) in St Petersburg soon after his arrival. The *pas de deux* from *Don Quixote*, now one of the most performed concert items, dates from Petipa's revival of his own work in St Petersburg in 1871. This production was extensively revised in the form of a grand spectacle complete with vision scene and marriage celebrations, foreshadowing in part the shape his later great classics would take.

Don Quixote was produced in parallel with *Coppelia* in Paris and together with Bournonville's work in Copenhagen is typical of the interest in national dances and exotic locations during this period.

Right: Peter Schaufuss in the National
Ballet of Canada production of La
Bayadere.

Left: The corps de ballet of the Royal
Ballet in the Kingdom of the Shades scene
of La Bayadere, which was the first major
production by Rudolf Nureyev after he
left Russia.

Petipa's next major work of which original choreography still exists was *La Bayadere*. The complete version is rarely seen outside Russia, but the last act, the Kingdom of the Shades scene, is much performed. It shows Petipa's total mastery of the simplest choreographic material. The opening, which is one of the most breathtaking of all scenes in ballet, consists of just two steps repeated by a seemingly endless line of ballerinas who slowly fill the stage. They move down a ramp at the back doing nothing more than a deep *arabesque penchée* and a back bend. This is perhaps one of the two peaks of his achievement, the other being the simple but devastating choreography for the Rose Adage in *The Sleeping Beauty*.

In Moscow, just one month after the premiere of *La Bayadere* in 1877, the resident choreographer Reisinger produced a ballet which was generally regarded as a failure. The score was badly arranged, the music completely misunderstood and the choreography undistinguished. The ballet was *Swan Lake*.

Petipa and the Classics

There is no historical reason for separating the three great classic ballets, *Swan Lake*, *The Sleeping Beauty* and *The Nutcracker*, into a category of their own. They were part of Petipa's developing brilliance and as such are direct descendants of his earlier work. They are, however, separated from the earlier works by their music.

La Bayadere, *The Pharaoh's Daughter* and *Don Quixote* had been created to music which was generally undistinguished, although much of it is still surprisingly

fresh today. It was the work of a resident composer prepared to compose to order for any occasion. The demands for new works by Petipa (his contract with the Imperial Theater demanded a new work each season) were great, but he managed to combine brilliant invention with careful use of formulae. His composers proved less inspired.

The controlling factor in the creation of all the works either choreographically or musically was the nature of the company. This was the Imperial Ballet, part of the Imperial Theater and as such part of the court of the tsar. Its administrators were civil servants, as were the dancers, and its ballets were prepared with the court in mind. The set-piece spectacle which Petipa devised became the accepted formula and it was rigidly adhered to. The formula itself was partially suggested by the intensely hierarchical nature of the company, as strict order of precedence had to be maintained. The prima ballerina reigned, similar to the tsar, and she was surrounded in descending order by the other ballerinas, the first soloists and then the different degrees of soloists down to the *corps de ballet*.

Petipa had to devise his choreography with this complex structure in mind, as each dancer required a solo or variation to suit her position. It would be unthinkable for a minor soloist to have a variation more brilliant than the prima ballerina and it was just as unthinkable for her partner to have more than a few steps of his own. The brilliant male solos we see today in these classics are later additions.

This was the cult of the ballerina all over again, but it did not have quite the same consequences as during the romantic age, other than to diminish male talent. This was particularly sad considering the strong tradition in Russia, a tradition which was to take a new lease of life during the following century.

The technique of the ballerina had continued to increase, building up to the age of the 32 *fouettés*, steps which were used for a particular dramatic reason at the time, but which have developed into a piece of pure circus over the years. Throughout Petipa's reign, as a result of the strong continuing tradition of teaching, a high proportion of his ballerinas were Russian and by the time he retired they had included such names as Kshessinska, Trefilova, Geltser, Egorova, Preobrajenskaya, Anna Pavlova and Tamara Karsavina. Some then went on to teach while others continued the dance tradition in the West following the Russian Revolution seven years after Petipa's death.

In spite of the wealth of native talent, Russia was still open to outside influence and welcomed ballerinas from Italy. Particularly important of these were Virginia Zucchi and Pierina Legnani.

Virginia Zucchi was born in Parma and received her early training in Milan. By the 1860s she was dancing throughout Italy, and later danced at La Scala, Milan where her roles included one in Ponchielli's *La Gioconda* to the ballet music now most commonly seen as part of Walt Disney's *Fantasia*, the *Dance of the Hours*. She danced in Covent Garden, London, before being engaged to dance in St Petersburg in 1885, not at the Imperial Theater, but in the pleasure gardens. She made such an impact that she was engaged by the Imperial Theater to dance at the Bolshoi in St Petersburg in Petipa's *Pharaoh's Daughter*. She made an even greater impact there and moved to the Maryinsky Theater. Her brilliant performances helped revive the flagging fortunes of the ballet before the great breakthrough of *The Sleeping Beauty*. She not only inspired younger dancers but attracted the interest of the young Alexander Benois who was an important figure in the next great age of the ballet.

Pierina Legnani joined the Maryinsky Theater in St Petersburg in 1893 where she first performed the 32 *fouettés* in *Cinderella*. Petipa used these when he came to produce *Swan Lake*, in which Legnani was to dance Odette-Odile. She also created another important role, that of *Raymonda* in the ballet which is now sadly neglected. The story is complicated, but the score by Glazunov is full of magnificent music.

Another guest ballerina from Italy was Carlotta Brianza who had been a pupil of Blasis in Milan. She made her debut in St Petersburg at the Summer Theater in 1887 and in 1890 created the role of Aurora in *The Sleeping Beauty*.

Left: The corps de ballet *of the National Ballet of Canada in* La Bayadere *with Karen Kain and Frank Augustyn as Nikiya and Solor.*

Below: Pierina Legnani and Sergei Legat in Camargo *at her benefit farewell performance in 1901.*

The Sleeping Beauty

Given the complexities of working within a civil service environment it often seems remarkable that Marius Petipa produced any ballets at all. There was inevitable intrigue between directors and assistant directors. Ballerinas had to be pandered to. Cohesive design was not possible since they insisted on wearing their own jewels, gifts from members of the court, to whom they would turn if they did not get their way.

By the time *The Sleeping Beauty* was being created, Petipa was nearly 70 and might have been expected to be past his peak. Tchaikovsky's one serious attempt at writing a ballet, *Swan Lake*, had been a dismal failure (from the audience point of view) and since that time he had written nothing for the dance.

The key figure in bringing together subject, choreographer and composer was I.A. Vsevolozhky, a nobleman who was director of the Imperial Theaters from 1881 to 1899. He was particularly cultured and a gifted designer. More importantly he had the vision of a complete ballet and believed in close collaboration between designer, choreographer and composer, an ideal long since forgotten. Furthermore he had given added life to the Russian ballet by engaging the Italian ballerinas as well as Enrico Cecchetti, who not only danced in *The Sleeping Beauty* but who became the most important teacher with the Imperial Theaters. He continued the tradition when he joined the Diaghilev Ballet and eventually his methods were codified by Cyril Beaumont, the eminent British critic.

Vsevolozhky also abolished the post of resident composer, so freeing the ballet from the strait-jacket of overused formulae. He first tried to interest Tchaikovsky in another ballet in 1886, based on *Ondine*, a product of the romantic age. Tchaikovsky, perhaps still affected by the failure of *Swan Lake*, was not inspired by the characters, although he had toyed with the idea of an opera on this subject. One of the themes he had sketched for this was used in one of the *pas de deux* in the second act of *Swan Lake*.

Bottom Left: Irina Kolpakova of the Kirov Ballet in one of her most famous roles, as Aurora in The Sleeping Beauty.

Bottom right: Yuri Soloviev, one of the greatest dancers of the role of the Bluebird in The Sleeping Beauty.

Right: Ekaterina Maximova in the Bolshoi version of The Sleeping Beauty.

In 1888 Vsevolozhky again approached Tchaikovsky, this time with the idea for a libretto based on the Perrault fairy-tale, *La Belle au Bois Dormant*. He already had a vision of the period, Louis XIV, and wanted both the design and music set within it. He had already conceived the wedding scene when fairy-tale characters – Tom Thumb, Cinderella, Little Red Riding Hood and many others – would attend the court. Tchaikovsky was more enthusiastic this time and agreed to write the music.

Working from Vsevolozhky's libretto, Petipa prepared his typically detailed notes for the composer. He had used this method before, but never with the inventive results produced by Tchaikovsky.

A typical scene as planned by Petipa shows the detail he went into; so detailed is it that it seems almost a miracle that Tchaikovsky could produce such free-flowing and glorious music. In the first act, following the prologue, Aurora celebrates her sixteenth birthday. All spindles have been banned from the land and old ladies with their knitting needles have been arrested. Aurora dances with the four princes who are seeking her hand in marriage. They present her with roses, which she gives to her parents.

'Suddenly Aurora sees an old woman who is beating the time of the dance with her knitting needles – 2/4 time. Gradually this changes to a waltz in 3/4 time. Aurora takes hold of the needles and expresses her delight – 24 bars waltz. A pause. Then she cries in pain. Blood flows – 8 strong bars in 4/4. She dances giddily, almost in a frenzy. She turns as if she has been bitten by a tarantula. She collapses. This will take 24 to 32 beats. At the end of this a few bars tremolo like cries of pain – Father! Mother! Then the old woman with the needles throws off her disguise.'

Above: Anneli Alhanko as Aurora in the controversial production of The Sleeping Beauty *by the Royal Swedish Ballet.*

Opposite: Lesley Collier and Anthony Dowell as Aurora and Florimund in the Royal Ballet The Sleeping Beauty.

Tchaikovsky worked out the prologue and the first and second acts before leaving for a concert tour in 1889 which took him to London. Here he saw a ballet performance at the Alhambra, where 33 years later Diaghilev's production of his ballet took place. The score was completed on the homeward journey and on the last page of the final draft he wrote: 'May 26 1889, 8pm. God be praised! Worked in all 10 days in October, three weeks in January and one week in May, a total of 40 days.' By the end of July he had finished the orchestration and pronounced it one of his best works.

When the ballet was in rehearsal Riccardo Drigo, who was to conduct the performance, was given a free hand to adjust the score to suit Petipa's requirements. He made many cuts, including the beautiful violin entr'acte which was thought to be too long. Nowadays it is included in productions either as a *pas de deux* for Aurora and her Prince (in the Ashton version) or as a solo for the Prince in the Hunting Scene (in the Nureyev version).

At the first performance in January 1890 Carlotta Brianza was Aurora, Pavel Gerdt was Prince Florimund and Enrico Cecchetti, whose range of technique and mime was prodigious, danced both Carabosse and the Bluebird. Carlotta Brianza was to dance the role of Carabosse some 31 years later in the production by Diaghilev in London. Vsevolozhky designed the costumes and the whole production stands as testimony to his vision. His faith in Tchaikovsky continued through *The Nutcracker* and finally to the act of rescuing the score of *Swan Lake*.

In spite of all these outstanding ingredients *The Sleeping Beauty* was not a great success at first. The audience found the music too symphonic after the simple rhythms of Minkus and the Tsar's comment was simply, 'Very nice.'

In spite of reservations *The Sleeping Beauty* was ultimately a success and almost half the ballet performances during that season were given over to it. Inevitably Vsevolozhky wanted a sequel which would match it and his choice of subject fell upon the story of *The Nutcracker and the Mouse-king* by E.T.A. Hoffmann who had been part of the romantic revolution. Why he chose this story is difficult to say, but it seems that his idea was based on the reworking by Dumas as *Casse Noisette*. According to Alexander Benois, however, Hoffmann was enjoying a period of approval by the St Petersburg intelligentsia.

Vsevolozhky wrote the libretto with Petipa in much the same way as he had for *The Sleeping Beauty* and Petipa then prepared the same detailed notes for Tchaikovsky. Tchaikovsky actively welcomed this detailed guidance, so different from the great mass of composers who would regard it as interference. It is even suggested by Russian writers that Tchaikovsky blamed the initial failure of *Swan Lake* on lack of such guidance from someone who understood the needs of dancing and that both *Beauty* and *Nutcracker* would have met a similar fate without Petipa's help. Indeed they might never have been written at all as *Nutcracker* was totally dependent on the success of *Beauty*.

Having written his detailed notes, Petipa went ahead and created steps before he received the finished score. If the two did not match he simply sent the music back for adjustment, but to be fair he did occasionally change his scenario. Tchaikovsky was entirely cooperative in this arrangement.

By 1891 Tchaikovsky's initial misgivings about the venture appeared to have

Below: The original Snowflakes in The Nutcracker *at the Maryinsky Theater, St Petersburg, 1892.*

grown worse. The libretto lacked the magic and grandeur of *Beauty*; indeed he found it bourgeois and this showed in his own estimation of his music, which he described as infinitely worse than *The Sleeping Beauty*.

Tchaikovsky finished the score in 1892 and without waiting for the production of the ballet produced the orchestral suite for performance in March 1892. It is hard to imagine how he persuaded Vsevolozhky to allow this or what his motives were for doing it. There is only one clue. When he was on his way to America the previous year he had passed through Paris and heard the 'divinely beautiful tone' of the celesta which had just been invented. He had decided to introduce the instrument to Russia and went to great lengths to keep his plans secret. Perhaps he feared news of it would leak out during rehearsals of the ballet, in which it was used for the variation of the Sugar Plum Fairy, and another Russian composer would steal his thunder.

Petipa started rehearsals in August so that the ballet would be ready for the winter season, but he was taken ill and the ballet was completed by his assistant Lev Ivanov. The publicity at the time credited Ivanov with all the choreography, but we can assume that, apart from the overall plan, Petipa was responsible for much of the Party Scene and some of the divertissements, while Ivanov choreographed the Snow Scene and the *grand pas de deux*. In view of his later achievements this would seem likely.

Lev Ivanov is a rather shadowy figure in the history of ballet in spite of a very distinguished career as dancer and teacher. For some time the view was taken that Petipa was jealous of his assistant (Ivanov was appointed to this post in 1885) which can only be justified on the grounds that Petipa did not like anyone encroaching into

Below: Rudolf Nureyev in his own production of The Nutcracker *in which Dr Drosselmeyer is transformed into the Nutcracker Prince in Clara's dream.*

Left: Natalia Bessmertnova and Mikhail Lavrovsky as Masha and her Prince in the Bolshoi Nutcracker.

territory he had held as his own for so long, especially someone of such obvious talent as Ivanov. It would be only human of Petipa to fear his younger assistant but if this was the complete truth, it is doubtful if Petipa would have entrusted Ivanov with such important work in *The Nutcracker* or even more work in *Swan Lake*. There is certainly no evidence of outside pressure for him to do so.

From a study of his career it would appear that Ivanov, in spite of great talent, lacked the drive and perhaps deviousness to make his way in the Imperial Theater. After his graduation in 1852 at the age of 16 he remained in the *corps de ballet* for six years despite his talent. He was an assiduous student, learning every role and never missing a rehearsal. This work stood him in good stead as his two great early opportunities involved dancing at short notice with little or, in one case, no rehearsal at all. He also started teaching at an early age, which again suggests a studious nature not interested in the rigors and politics of performing.

During his lifetime he received no credit and, it would seem, very little financial reward. Even after the success of his choreography for the dances in the opera *Prince Igor* and for both *The Nutcracker* and *Swan Lake*, he died poor and forgotten in 1901.

The Nutcracker was premiered on 18 December 1892. It was not a success. Antonietta dell'Era was not liked as the Sugar Plum Fairy and the production was bad. The décor, according to Alexander Benois, who designed similar charming productions himself in later years, was a complete disaster.

The original Petipa/Ivanov version is almost completely lost. The best we can say is that some versions of the *grand pas de deux* bear a slight resemblance to Ivanov's original. However, the glorious score has guaranteed the ballet a long life and with different choreographies it is now perhaps the most performed of all ballets.

Below: Adyrkhanova and Bogatryev in the Bolshoi Swan Lake.

The following year Tchaikovsky died of cholera at the early age of 53. His attempts at writing for the ballet were not generally successful in his lifetime. Even *The Sleeping Beauty* had been misunderstood and *The Nutcracker* hardly acclaimed. His death did, however, act in part as a catalyst to bring the score of *Swan Lake* back into the theater.

It was decided to stage a performance in his memory and the score for the long forgotten *Swan Lake* was suggested as a subject. Lev Ivanov choreographed the second act at the memorial performance and the entire ballet was revived the following year at the Maryinsky Theater, St Petersburg. Petipa supervised the whole production and choreographed the 'court' acts, while Ivanov choreographed the 'white' lakeside acts. It was a success in spite of the fact that its construction broke new ground for Russian ballet at the time. The romantic second act with its high drama was a far cry from the court formalities of *The Sleeping Beauty* and other works. The grand court scene of the third act was not the peak of the ballet because the action quickly returns to the drama of the lovers by the lake.

The division of the choreographic work reflects the differing talents of Petipa and Ivanov. Petipa was at home at court. He could arrange perfectly the niceties of the formal dances both for the Prince's coming of age in the first act and the national dances of the third. He used Legnani's ability to perform 32 *fouettés* to brilliant dramatic effect as Odile, the Black Swan, mesmerizes Siegfried into thinking she is Odette. Ivanov excelled at the softer and more delicately dramatic 'white' acts. His work on the Snow Scene in *The Nutcracker* is reflected here and his intimate understanding of the two lovers in their second act *pas de deux* must surely come from his own introspective nature.

Right: Merle Park and Anthony Dowell as Odile and Siegfried in the third act of the Royal Ballet Swan Lake.

Left: Marilyn Rowe in the Australian Ballet Swan Lake.

Overleaf: Natalia Bessmertnova and Mikhail Lavrovsky in the second and third acts of the Bolshoi Swan Lake.

Above: The decorative corps de ballet *of the Bolshoi in* The Goldfish, *1903.*

After *Swan Lake* in 1 [illegible] major ballet before his retirement in 1903. This was *Raymonda* in 1898. The score was commissioned from Alexander Glazunov, thought by many to be the natural successor to Tchaikovsky. However, he did not work to order with quite the same ease and there were difficulties during the creation of the ballet. Whatever these were, the resulting score is full of magnificent music. Unfortunately the story was extremely complicated and frequently silly, which has hampered all recent attempts at revival. The third act is often performed as a divertissement, but perhaps the most widespread version is the dance suite choreographed by George Balanchine. Rudolf Nureyev attempted to make some sense of the story, but the tale of Raymonda, of the Saracen who tries to abduct her while her beloved is away at the crusades and their happy reuniting, defeated even him.

By the beginning of the twentieth century the classical ballet was already past its peak of achievement. The ballerina reigned supreme with both technical and artistic mastery, but her partner was still subservient. The great ballets had been created and Petipa produced no more successes. The ballet was still firmly part of the Imperial Court. It was inevitable that there would be signs of revolt against the system. Artists, designers, composers and choreographers began to feel the need to explore new fields.

The first stirrings of the modern dance movement had taken place and the apostle of change, Isadora Duncan, appeared in Russia in 1907 just two years after the apostle of change in the classical ballet had created his first ballet. Mikhail Fokine, through his choreography, was drawn into a circle of ballet activists set on change. They included Alexander Benois, Leon Bakst and Serge Diaghilev.

Right: Anthony Dowell as the Spirit of the Rose.

The Diaghilev Era

To unravel the roots of what was to become known as the Diaghilev period of ballet, which we define as extending from his first Paris season in 1909 to his death in 1929, we must look back to St Petersburg and Moscow in the 1890s.

Serge Pavlovich Diaghilev was born in Perm in 1872. He came from a family of country nobility rather than the fashionable city nobility more immediate to the court of the tsar, and he tried hard to compensate for this. His early ambition was to be a composer, but through family pressure he went to St Petersburg to study law.

Once in St Petersburg he came into contact with a lively group of young artists, one of whose main interests was the ballet. The young leader of the group was an art student, Alexander Benois, whose interest in the ballet had been fired at an early age by Virginia Zucchi and there are stories that his infatuation had once led him to lay his coat on the road for her to step on as she entered her carriage. Quite why ballerinas have this sort of effect on their followers is hard to explain and worthy of a study in itself. Taglioni's followers in Russia cooked one of her ballet slippers and ate it with a sauce, while her fans in Vienna unhooked her carriage and pulled her through the streets.

Left: Rudolf Nureyev as the Golden Slave in Scheherazade.

Above: Per Arthur Segestrom as the Poet in Les Sylphides.

Right: Ann Jenner as the Firebird.

The group, which included the young Jewish artist Leon Bakst, was heavily biased toward art and design. They were interested in the use of original painting, or at least designs by easel painters, for the theater, to replace hack designs by the state-employed, resident designers. They found that many of their ideals were being used in a private theater company organized by the rich merchant Mamantov in Moscow. He used painters such as Korovin and Golovin, both of whom collaborated with Diaghilev when he finally launched his company.

When Diaghilev first came into contact with the group he was not immediately welcomed as he did not have any specific talent. He still dabbled with composition, but Rimsky-Korsakov is reported as having told him that he did not have an original talent. His retort that 'I will be remembered when you are forgotten' was very much in character, but he did not bear a grudge and used Rimsky-Korsakov's music in later years.

His quality as a leader and innovator found expression when he stimulated the group to produce a magazine, *The World of Art*, in 1898. This proved not only influential in the Russian art world, but gave the group an entry to the closed world of the Imperial Theater. Alongside this venture Diaghilev organized art exhibitions, perhaps a suggestion of his future destiny as an impresario.

Diaghilev had not been particularly interested in the ballet other than as a vehicle for design. *The Sleeping Beauty* made no particular impression on him, which is a reminder that in spite of the music and some glorious choreography, the *form* of the work was sterile. The arrangement of the acts was simply the nineteenth-century equivalent of the court entertainments two centuries earlier. *Raymonda* made a greater impression, in spite of its ridiculous libretto. It appeared in the same year as the first publication of *The World of Art*. Clearly by this time interest as an observer was being strengthened by interest as a possible participant.

The World of Art included among its contributors Prince Volkonsky, a man of refined taste, an expert on several aspects of the theater and perhaps most importantly, a progressive. He was impressed by the activities of the group and his appointment as Director of the Imperial Theaters in 1899 opened the way for change.

Volkonsky was part of the establishment and knew the perils of trying to change too much too fast. To introduce the group into the theater he gave Diaghilev the job of editing the *Annual* of the Imperial Theaters. Seeing their chance, the Diaghilev-Benois circle pushed forward too rapidly and pressed Volkonsky into allowing them to organize the new production of *Sylvia* as a vehicle for their ideals. He agreed and in 1900 they started work. Diaghilev oversaw the production and the designs were prepared by members of the group.

It must be remembered that at this time Diaghilev had only the lowest position in the Imperial Theaters and it seemed almost inevitable that established civil servants would protest at the power he was given. In an attempt to smooth things over Volkonsky suggested that the production should simply be announced under the name of the directorate, and the group would be allowed to continue with their work. Diaghilev would not agree and tried several means, not all of them particularly honest, to keep the production in his own name. He even appealed to the Tsar, but without result. Volkonsky continued his efforts to make Diaghilev see that it would be wise to allow the members of his group to infiltrate the theater slowly, but he would not compromise. He was then dismissed by the Tsar and banned from the Imperial Theater.

It was not long before Volkonsky himself was forced to resign. He fell foul of the prima ballerina assoluta, Mathilde Kshessinska, who had a close relationship with the Imperial family. After the revolution she lived in France and married the Grand Duke Andrey. Teliakovsky, the new director, was not sympathetic to the progressive cause and Benois was eventually only able to go ahead with *Le Pavillon d'Armide* because Teliakovsky was on vacation.

This ballet is important for it brought together for the first time important elements

Prince Volkonsky

which later fused to become the Diaghilev Ballet. When Benois first suggested the subject, Teliakovsky was not enthusiastic. He wanted waltzes. He did, however, continue to deal with Benois and other members of the group.

In the later ballets of Marius Petipa, who resigned, disillusioned, in 1903, Mikhail Fokine appeared as a young soloist. He had no contact with the Diaghilev group in this period and continued on his own way as dancer and teacher at the Imperial School. His first experiments at choreography were made for the annual displays of the senior pupils; from these he progressed to occasional ballets for charity performances – the atmosphere at the Imperial Theater allowed no room for his work. Among his early pieces was a moving solo, the significance of which he can hardly have realized. This was *The Swan*, created for one of the most promising young ballerinas of the Maryinsky, Anna Pavlova.

When Benois first had the idea for *Le Pavillon d'Armide*, based on a story by Gautier, he had commissioned a score from the composer Alexander Tcherepnin. Fokine heard about the project and produced one scene for a performance by his pupils. Kuprensky, the director of productions, liked it and arranged for a production of the whole ballet at the Maryinsky in Teliakovsky's absence. He encouraged both Benois and Fokine, but his attitude changed on Teliakovsky's return. Fortunately Benois was much more level-headed than Diaghilev had been in similar trying circumstances and work went ahead.

Obstacles were still to be surmounted and one week before the premiere, Kshessinska refused to dance in it. Anna Pavlova stepped into her place although she must have been aware that the Directorate would not approve. Finally the ballet was announced; it was to *follow* a performance of *Swan Lake*, which would have effectively robbed it of an audience. Benois protested publicly and the ballet was postponed until 25 November 1907.

Now that Fokine had been drawn into the Diaghilev circle the group was complete.

Diaghilev's organizing urge following his departure from the Imperial Theater, was soon channelled into new ventures. In 1907 he presented concerts of Russian music in Paris and in 1908 brought a whole production, *Boris Godunov*, with Chaliapine in the title role. These ventures were backed by the Grand Duke Vladimir, who had been interested in the activities of the group for some time but apparently had not been able to help them within Russia.

His patronage was useful to Diaghilev in providing a base at the Hermitage Theater in St Petersburg for the storage of costumes and scenery, at least until the time of his death. This played havoc with Diaghilev's plans for an even grander season in Paris. Kshessinka once more was the center of trouble because she did not want to share the limelight with Anna Pavlova, and Diaghilev lost the use of the Hermitage. The season did, however, take place, but with different patrons in both Russia and France. It did not break much new ground. *Le Pavillon d'Armide* had been performed in St Petersburg. Fokine revived two ballets which he had already produced for charity performances: *Chopiniana* which we know of as *Les Sylphides*, and *Une Nuit d'Egypte* renamed *Cléopatre*. The program also included the Polovtsian Dances from the opera *Prince Igor* with new choreography by Fokine to replace the original by Ivanov.

The season opened on 19 May 1909 at the Chatelet Theater. The Diaghilev Ballet was born. Paris went wild with excitement. The first night was a spectacular occasion and the audience included glittering socialites, the most beautiful actresses of the day, painters and musicians. They were astounded by the techniques and personality of the Russian dancers. Adolph Bolm led the Polovtsian Warriors with a virility never seen on the Paris ballet stage. Tamara Karsavina and Anna Pavlova had great personal successes, but the triumph of the evening was the performance by the young Vaslav Nijinsky. Anna Pavlova danced only a few more performances for Diaghilev before forming her own company. The partnership of Nijinsky and Karsavina became legendary.

Serafina Astafieva, who became an important teacher in London and numbered Markova, Fonteyn and Dolin among her pupils, as Cleopatra.

Left: Tania Bari and the Ballet of the Twentieth Century in Maurice Béjart's Rite of Spring.

Above: Valery Panov, one of the Kirov's outstanding character dancers, as Petrouchka in America.

After this triumphant success another season was planned for the following year. Diaghilev had noticed that the refined Parisian audience had been particularly captivated by the glorious, exotic colors and settings as well as by the brilliant performers, and he set about creating a program which would repeat this success.

Although about to embark on the second season there was still no permanent Diaghilev company. Both his dancers and his choreographers were members of the Imperial Ballet who could only dance for him during their vacations. The *corps de ballet* needed such vacation work to supplement their low salaries, but Diaghilev had to contend with other demands placed on his ballerinas who were increasingly securing engagements elsewhere. The only permanent group was the expanded Diaghilev-Benois circle.

Diaghilev devoted his time in these early years to organization, fund raising and to some extent being responsible for the music. Benois acted as artistic director, devising themes for ballets and either designing or supervising the designs for them. Leon Bakst, although primarily a designer, contributed general ideas about presentation and subjects. Diaghilev, with his interest in composition, must have realized that the missing person in this group was a composer to match the talents of the choreographer, dancers and designers. When planning the 1910 season, he discovered Igor Stravinsky.

The repertoire Diaghilev planned for the 1910 season included one classic, *Giselle*, and three new works. These were *The Firebird, Carnaval* and *Scheherazade. Giselle*

did not find great favor. The Parisian audience wanted the colorful, the exotic, the Russian. Even *Carnaval* must have appeared tame to them, but Nijinsky's performance as Harlequin, with Karsavina as Columbine, must have been very moving, judging from photographs. *Scheherazade* was more to the taste of the audience. Based on an idea by Benois (but credited to Bakst) taken from the *Thousand and One Nights* stories, the combination of Bakst's gorgeous décor, Fokine's choreography and Rimsky-Korsakov's music is a powerful one. Ida Rubenstein played Zobeide, the Shah's favorite, but unfaithful, wife, and Nijinsky created another sensation with his sensual interpretation of the Golden Slave.

The Firebird was by far the most important work performed during the season. It is a mysterious Russian folk-tale, brilliantly evoked by Fokine and Golovin. The idea for a ballet of this type came from Diaghilev. He had given his audience the excitement of *Prince Igor* during the first season and felt that they were in the mood for more Russian folklore.

For the new production Fokine prepared his own libretto based on many Russian tales, most notably those of Afanasiev, which featured the Firebird. Another member of the group, Remizov, who specialized in folklore, contributed some of the details of

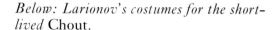

Left: Leon Bakst's exotic costume design for Potiphar's wife in The Legend of Joseph.

monsters and spirits. Then came the problem of the score, about which there has developed a mythology as exotic as the Firebird. Diaghilev apparently commissioned a score from Liadov, his former professor of harmony, in 1909, telling him that he wished to present the ballet nine months later in May 1910. It appears that Liadov accepted, but was not used to such tight schedules. There is a famous story of Diaghilev meeting Liadov some time later and asking him how the score was progressing. 'Very well,' said Liadov, 'You will have it shortly. I have just bought the ruled paper.' Diaghilev was forced to switch composers and this time chose Tcherepnin, who had been instrumental in bringing together Fokine and Benois. He was enthusiastic, but did not produce a score. The final choice fell on Igor Stravinsky.

After problems similar to the commissioning of the score, the designs of the ballet were eventually completed by Golovin, with the addition of dresses by Bakst for the Firebird herself and the enchanted princess. The designs most commonly used today, as in the production by the Royal Ballet, for instance, are based on those for

Diaghilev's revival of the ballet in 1926 by Gontcharova. Stravinsky in later years had a strong preference for George Balanchine's production of the ballet to the shorter orchestral suite, with designs by Georges Chagall.

Anna Pavlova, who had worked so closely with Fokine and was Stravinsky's favorite dancer, was the first choice for the role of the Firebird, but she apparently did not approve of Stravinsky's music. So the role went to Tamara Karsavina, with the Prince being performed by Fokine himself. He had partnered her for her debut at the Maryinsky eight years before, in 1902.

The season was another remarkable success. Diaghilev's problems regarding dancers were highlighted when the public demanded extra performances of *The Firebird*. Tamara Karsavina had agreed to an engagement in London, so he was forced to find another ballerina. His choice fell upon Lydia Lopokova who had created the role of Columbine in *Carnaval* in Berlin prior to the Paris season. She did not become a permanent member of the company, but was always popular. She went on to create such roles as the Can-Can dancer in *La Boutique Fantasque* and the Milkmaid and Tango Dancer in *Façade* and to marry the British economist John Maynard Keynes.

Such problems and such successes hardened Diaghilev's resolve to make his company permanent. Fokine became his ballet master and Nijinsky and Karsavina his principal dancers. At exactly the right moment Nijinsky was involved in a scandal at the Maryinsky and forced to resign. Perhaps it is unfair to suggest that Diaghilev encouraged him to behave in an arrogant manner, but it is a possibility. Nijinsky had appeared in *Giselle* wearing the wrong costume and was ordered to apologize for offending the Dowager Empress. He refused to do so. His expulsion was automatic and he was free to dance for Diaghilev. Fokine and Karsavina agreed to join the company (keeping some connections with the Maryinsky, as ballerinas were only required to give a certain number of performances each season and could arrange their own dates). Enrico Cecchetti joined the company as teacher.

Diaghilev found the company a home in Monte Carlo and they set to work on the new productions for the 1911 season, which would take them to London for the first time. These included two which were to become mainstays of the modern repertoire: *Le Spectre de la Rose* and *Petrouchka*.

Fokine's *Le Spectre de la Rose* is really an extended *pas de deux* and will forever be associated with Nijinsky and Karsavina. There have been many revivals with dancers of considerable eminence, but the magic of the work has proved consistently elusive, as elusive as the spirit of the rose the young girl brings home from her first ball.

The idea for the ballet came from Jean-Louis Vaudoyer, a critic for *La Revue de Paris*. As he was making notes about the productions of the Russian Ballet in 1909 and 1910, he wrote the famous lines of Gautier at the head of an item about *Carnaval*:

> *Je suis le spectre de la rose,*
> *Que tu portais hier au bal.*

In his own account of how this germ of an idea developed, Vaudoyer tells how the memory of the Russian dancers was still fresh long after they had left. He also remembered Gautier's love of the music of Weber (harking back to the romantic age) and in particular the *Invitation to the Waltz* which Berlioz had orchestrated.

Putting these thoughts together Vaudoyer wrote to Bakst suggesting the idea for the ballet. There was no answer, but the following May Diaghilev sent a note inviting him and his friends to Monte Carlo to see the final rehearsals for the ballet. The letter had not gone unheeded. As the ballet involved only two dancers, Fokine had started rehearsals in St Petersburg. According to Karsavina in her delightful book of memoirs, *Theatre Street*, Fokine made the ballet in one easy flight of inspiration, taking perhaps no more than four rehearsals. It received its first performance on 6 June 1911 and was an unqualified success. Nijinsky astounded with his uncanny incarnation of the spirit of the rose and by the fantastic leap with which he left the stage.

Carla Fracci with John Gilpin in Le Spectre de la Rose.

Above: The fairground scene from Petrouchka *in the Royal Ballet version with Nureyev as Petrouchka.*

Just one week later *Petrouchka* received its premiere. This is perhaps the most perfect combination of all the artistic ideals which the original Diaghilev-Benois group and Fokine as choreographer represented. The elements of the production are so perfectly blended that individual ones cannot be isolated. Even the demanding role of Petrouchka himself, which requires a truly great artist, does not stand out from the overall production.

So close was the collaboration between the designer, choreographer and composer that it is difficult to unravel how the ballet came about. Stravinsky had the vision of a short piano piece picturing a duel between a puppet and the orchestra, but had already moved on to another major project, *The Rite of Spring*, before he wrote it down. Diaghilev saw the possibilities of this piece as a ballet and asked Benois to develop it. Benois was still smarting and generally uncooperative following the argument over the creation of *Scheherazade*, but the idea appealed to him and brought back childhood memories of the old fairs in St Petersburg. He then worked with Stravinsky on the detailed scenario, with all members of the group contributing their ideas for characters such as the coachmen and grooms, fantastic animals and street dancers. Benois continued to supervise the details of the production although Fokine was responsible for all the dances.

In performance Nijinsky added an element of pathos perhaps even greater than that imagined by the ballet's creators. It gave him his greatest role as the sad puppet figure, hopelessly in love with the stupid ballerina and ill-treated by both the Showman and the Moor. The way he identified himself with the role has macabre overtones in the context of his own life story.

Vaslav Nijinsky

The story of Vaslav Nijinsky is inextricably tied up with both Serge Diaghilev personally and the Diaghilev Ballet. He was born in Kiev in 1888. Both his parents were dancers, his mother having studied in the ballet school in Warsaw and subsequently joined the company there. His father, too, was Polish, though his high cheekbones and slanted eyes suggested Tartar blood. He was an outstanding dancer and also a gifted choreographer. Together Nijinsky's parents toured the length and breadth of Russia (his sister Bronislav was born in Minsk), taking their children with them.

Nijinsky's father eventually left home to start another family with his mistress. His mother then gave up the stage and settled with the children in St Petersburg. Nijinsky had an older brother who was simple-minded, but it appears that this was more likely the result of a fall and not, as might be thought in view of Nijinsky's future, the result of any hereditary trait.

In 1898 Nijinsky's mother took him to the Imperial Ballet School in St Petersburg, as much out of financial need (if he was accepted he would be fully looked after) as any urge to carry on the family tradition in the dance. The initial impression he gave was not good. His oriental looks and unusual physique did not mark him out as a natural dancer, but the teacher of the boys, Nicholas Legat, noticed him and took him into the school, predicting even at that age a special future for him.

While at the school Nijinsky made good progress and along with other students took part in ballets such as *The Little Humpbacked Horse*, still a popular favorite in Russia, and *The Nutcracker*. He first crossed the path of Mikhail Fokine while still at school, taking part, and being noticed in, Fokine's ballet based on the Ivanov version of *Acis and Galatea*. It was soon apparent that this student was going to be an outstanding dancer.

His graduation in April 1907 was also a success and he was congratulated by no less a person than Kshessinska, who indicated that she would like him to partner her. He did indeed do this soon after when she commanded his presence to partner her at a performance during army maneuvers attended by the Tsar and the Grand Dukes. During the following season he danced many major roles, in spite of the fact that he was still in the *corps de ballet*. They included the *pas de deux* from *Paquita* as well as the *pas de deux* from both *La Fille Mal Gardée* and *Giselle*. The latter (probably the peasant *pas de deux* and not that from the second act) he danced with Karsavina, marking the start of a glorious partnership.

It was not long before Nijinsky met Diaghilev, who had of course seen him dance at the Maryinsky. Nijinsky did not take to him at first sight, but the relationship developed into a deep personal one. From his diary it is also clear that Nijinsky was aware that Diaghilev's tuition and encouragement could make him the greatest dancer of the age. It was a relationship which produced many masterpieces of lasting quality.

After he was dismissed from the Maryinsky and joined the Diaghilev enterprise as the principal dancer, it was not long before his mind turned to choreography. Diaghilev encouraged him, for more than one reason. He was growing tired of Fokine and saw the next phase of the company's development embodied in Nijinsky the choreographer, as well as Nijinsky the dancer.

With his first ballet, *Afternoon of a Faun*, Nijinsky broke new ground immediately. Given his technique it might have been expected that he would produce purely classical works, but as it turned out he abandoned classical principles and devised an entirely personal style, based on the two-dimensional figures on Greek friezes. This style derived from the methods of Emile-Jacques Dalcroze who had devised the system of eurythmics to help his students with musical rhythms, not dance. Diaghilev

Nijinsky as the Golden Slave in Fokine's Scheherazade.

and Nijinsky had visited him and both the style and the subject derived from this visit.

The premiere of his ballet took place at the Chatelet Theater on 29 May 1912, featuring Nelidova and Nijinsky. It was applauded by a few, but booed, hissed and jeered at by many. Diaghilev, with brilliant self-possession, immediately ordered the ballet to be performed again.

Nijinsky followed this ballet with *Jeux*, which broke further new ground in that the characters at a house party wore modern dress and the gestures were based on real actions. By the following year he was working on perhaps his greatest achievement as creator and innovator, *The Rite of Spring*. The choreographic ideas in this ballet were entirely his own, but to help him unravel the complex rhythms of Stravinsky's powerful score he had the aid of Marie Rambert. The primitive rites he depicted for the Russian peasants, together with the advanced music, produced one of the greatest riots ever seen in a theater. The dancers could not hear the music and Nijinsky had to beat out the complicated rhythms in the wings.

Diaghilev had plans for more ballets by Nijinsky, but when the company went on tour to South America in 1913, Nijinsky married Romola Pulsky, a Polish dancer with the company. Marie Rambert has given a most moving account of this brief romance, which may well mark Nijinsky's gesture of independence. Diaghilev dispensed with his services immediately and Nijinsky appeared with the company on only a few more occasions, usually following pressure from impresarios.

Nijinsky alone, and with Karsavina, in Le Spectre de la Rose.

Nijinsky appeared in London with his own company in 1914, but during the Great War he was interned as an alien in Hungary. Diaghilev's efforts secured his release and he joined the company again in 1916 for the New York season. He took over the direction of the company when Diaghilev left for Europe and worked on his last choreography, *Tyl Eulenspiegel*. It enjoyed some success, but the illness which was to develop into madness was progressing. He briefly visited Diaghilev in Spain before joining the company for their second American tour. He gave his last performance in Buenos Aires on 26 September 1917, when he danced *Le Spectre de la Rose* and *Petrouchka*.

Nijinsky was just 29 and had danced for the last time. With his devoted wife Romola he moved to Switzerland. There he planned to give a recital for the Red Cross. He would not discuss the details, but costumes were made and a pianist ready. On the day of the recital in January 1919, it was still not clear what the pianist was to perform. Nijinsky wore practice clothes and asked the pianist to play Chopin or, according to different reports, Schumann. He made a few disjointed gestures to the music. Next he danced a more energetic solo in the style for which he was famous. Then he said he was tired. His wife Romola remembers his dancing being brilliant, but it reminded her of the scene from *Petrouchka* when the puppet tries to escape his fate.

Soon after this Nijinsky was declared insane and spent the next 31 years in sanatoria. He and Romola were interned in Hungary again during the Second World War, but escaped to Austria before coming to Britain in 1947. He died in the Welbeck Hotel on Easter Saturday, 8 April 1950. Following his funeral in St James', Spanish Place, he was buried in the St Marylebone cemetery. In 1953 his body was transferred to Paris and buried near the grave of Auguste Vestris.

Maurice Béjart produced a whole evening's spectacle based on the life of Nijinsky. Right: Nijinsky (Jorge Donn) being put through the hoop by the Ringmaster who is clearly intended to be Diaghilev. Below: Nijinsky surrounded by the characters he made famous – the Golden Slave, Petrouchka, the Spirit of the Rose and the Faun.

Following the success of *Petrouchka* it might seem odd that Diaghilev should have already been making plans to oust Fokine and for Nijinsky to take up choreography.

Fokine had been a romanticist born out of classicism. He, almost single-handedly, had re-established ballet after it had fossilized into the court spectacle. He had broken away from the compulsory formula of the three- or four-act ballet and had treated the *corps de ballet* as a living part of the ballet and not a decoration. In many ways he had returned to the long forgotten traditions of Vigano and Perrot. Perhaps, however, like so many revolutionaries, he could not see when he had become the establishment. He was so engrossed in his own theories that he did not feel the need to change and move forward himself.

Diaghilev, being a mixture of artistic and commercial genius, had to be aware of these changes. Even so the way he effected the change was a little suspect. Perhaps he felt a need to dispense with Fokine's services because he was not totally a Diaghilev creation. This may be one explanation, but he did not behave this way toward dancers and designers of established reputation. He obviously had the difficult task of balancing the fact that Fokine's ideas were rapidly going out of date with the hopes he had for Nijinsky.

Fokine planned a new production for the company, *Daphnis and Chloe*, but Diaghilev interfered and would not allow sufficient time for rehearsal. He gave all his energies to helping Nijinsky with his work on *Afternoon of a Faun*. Not surprisingly *Daphnis and Chloe* was not finished in time for production and Diaghilev pressed Fokine to cancel it. Fokine refused and managed to complete it.

Fokine's eventual departure did not cause the company immediate trouble. Nijinsky was satisfying the intellectual side of Diaghilev, as well as providing sufficient

Bottom left: Margot Fonteyn and Christopher Gable in Frederick Ashton's version of Daphnis and Chloe.

Bottom right: Marilyn Rowe and Gary Norman of the Australian Ballet in Jerome Robbins' version of Afternoon of a Faun.

public interest in the company. *Rite of Spring* was almost as great a blending of all the elements as *Petrouchka*, a fact often lost in the drama and excitement of its reception, and *Afternoon of a Faun* had its scandalous ending about which there has been controversy ever since.

Soon, however, Diaghilev was to find himself without a choreographer through his break with Nijinsky and, through the advent of war, temporarily without a company. He did have one last season in the year war broke out, when he presented a sumptuous production of Rimsky-Korsakov's *Golden Cockerel* by Fokine, designed by Gontcharova. Karsavina was the beautiful Queen of Shemakhan and Enrico Cecchetti the Astrologer. Fokine also choreographed *The Legend of Joseph* with music by Richard Strauss and it was in this ballet that Diaghilev introduced his latest discovery, the 17-year-old Leonide Massine. Diaghilev always had an eye to the future.

To find sufficient bookings to keep such an enormous undertaking on the road in the early years of the war was well-nigh impossible and the company was forced to disband. In 1915, however, Diaghilev was invited to bring his company to New York and he made great efforts to bring together the dispersed dancers and to get Nijinsky released from internment in Hungary. Karsavina had returned home to St Petersburg and was expecting a child, so the company was headed by Lydia Lopokova who had stood in for her once before. Nijinsky was eventually released but reached New York too late for the first season. He was present, however, for the second season at the Metropolitan Opera House and danced brilliantly, although members of the company noticed a change of attitude, which they put down to implacable hostility toward Diaghilev.

Diaghilev was of course polite to both Nijinsky and his wife; he had to be, for the company depended on them. Diaghilev had already seen that the American audiences expected a first-rate show. After all, they had already seen Anna Pavlova. But he did not have to encourage Nijinsky's choreography any more, by then he was interested only in furthering Massine's career. The strain was, nevertheless, still there and for the second visit to America, in 1917, the impresario Otto Kahn arranged for the company to travel without Diaghilev. The artistic direction was to be shared by Nijinsky and Adolph Bolm, the fine dancer who had made such a strong impression in *Prince Igor*. As co-director Nijinsky was able to produce his ballet, *Tyl Eulenspiegel* and, in fact, this was the first new ballet of importance created since his dismissal years earlier.

Diaghilev's interest now centered completely around Massine, who was being groomed to create the stream of ballets which would restore the Diaghilev Ballet after the Great War. The Russian Revolution of 1917 cut many dancers and teachers off from their country and Diaghilev was able to strengthen his company considerably. It visited London in 1918 and gave one-act ballets as part of a variety bill at Sir Oswald Stoll's Coliseum, before presenting a ballet season at the Alhambra. It was to stay in London continuously, with only a short break in Manchester, for almost a year.

Massine was studying drama in the Imperial School in Moscow and about to graduate as an actor when Diaghilev first discovered him in 1913. Although the division between actors and dancers at the school was not rigid, he had relatively little experience in dance. Diaghilev, however, clearly thought he had in him the ability to replace Nijinsky as both dancer and choreographer and invited him to join the company.

Although it was an unrealistic aim, Massine nevertheless made enormous progress following his touching performance in *The Legend of Joseph* in 1914. Within three years he had embarked on a major work, although he had taken his first choreographic steps in 1915 with a short suite of Russian folk dances. In 1917 the company presented *The Good Humoured Ladies* on their return from America. It was based on an eighteenth-century comedy by Goldoni with music from the same period by Scarlatti. It is a charming tale which has withstood recent revival, but it has not entered any repertory on a permanent basis. The cast included Lydia Lopokova and Massine, together with Tchernicheva, Woizikowski and Idzikowski, who were so important to the ballet tradition in Britain and Australia after Diaghilev's death.

In the summer of the same year Massine produced *Parade*, which received its premiere in Paris. It had a scenario by Jean Cocteau, who had been an ardent follower of the Russian ballet from the first season. His influence was enormous, but not always for the best. There is a school of thought which blamed his influence for the later policies of the Diaghilev company which led to what has become known as the 'Cocktail' period.

Parade represented a complete break from the policy of the pre-war company and marked the beginning of great involvement with the leading painters and designers of the day. The score, by Erik Satie, included unusual instruments (including type-writers) and the décor and costumes were by Picasso in his Cubist style.

By now Nijinsky had danced for the last time and the full burden of creation had long been on Massine. In 1918 the company was still having difficulties as a result of the war and spent some time in Spain. Fortunately, Diaghilev secured an engagement in London at the Alhambra and it was here, in 1919, that the premiere of *La Boutique Fantasque* took place.

This has proved to be one of Massine's most lasting and popular ballets, and is constantly revived. He based the scenario on an old Viennese ballet which had been performed at the Maryinsky in 1902. Although it was essentially a divertissement with only a slight theme – dolls who come alive at night – it was full of comic invention. Again Massine was featured with Lopokova, in the brilliant Can-Can, ·something common to most of his ballets. This has turned out to be one of their

Above: Alexandra Danilova and Leonide Massine as the Can-Can Dancers in Massine's La Boutique Fantasque.

weaknesses. The principal role is invariably so tied up with the highly idiosyncratic style of the choreography that it is very difficult for other dancers to capture that special brilliance. This was to prove so, yet again, with his next ballet, *The Three Cornered Hat*.

The time Massine had spent with Diaghilev and the company in Spain was not wasted. They had studied Spanish dance and Massine had absorbed it perfectly and was able to translate it into a balletic style. He had been taught by a Spanish dancer, Felix, who came to London with the company, apparently under the impression that he was to dance the leading role. Felix had improvised a *farucca* which was to be the highpoint of the ballet, but when he found that it was to be danced by Massine himself he became mentally unhinged and sadly was to remain so.

The music was by Manuel de Falla and once more the costumes and scenery were by Picasso. This ballet also brought Karsavina back to London, where she had been a most popular favorite.

At this time Massine was the only choreographer with the company and by the age of 23 he had created seven ballets, mostly of a very high standard. The strain must have been enormous and he inevitably became set in his own successful mold. In

1920 he created *Pulcinella*. It enjoyed some success and Stravinsky's music, reworking and echoing themes of Pergolesi, was particularly inventive. At the end of the same year he produced, at Diaghilev's insistence, a new version of *The Rite of Spring*. Diaghilev's motives here were probably mixed. Possibly he wanted to erase all traces of Nijinsky, for he could have arranged a revival of that production. As it was, Massine's version broke away from the strong peasant rituals of Nijinsky's production and had a more abstract theme.

By now, as seems almost inevitable, Massine's relations with Diaghilev had deteriorated and in 1921 he left. He was to return briefly six years later in the 'cocktail' period to choreograph *Le Pas d'Acier* with music by Prokofiev and *Ode*, interesting as an experiment in stagecraft, to a score by Nicholas Nabokov.

Following Massine's departure, Diaghilev was left without a choreographer and he did not find one until he realized the potential of Bronislav Nijinska, sister of Vaslav. He had many good dancers who could take over Massine's roles, but was in need of new ballets. Only one ballet, *Chout*, conceived by the designer Larionov in collaboration with a dancer, Slavinsky, was produced before his ideas for a large-scale production crystallized.

Following the successful summer season in London, Diaghilev agreed to return later in the year with a new production and the hope that this one ballet would run, like a popular musical, for a very long time. His choice fell upon *The Sleeping Beauty* and Sir Oswald Stoll, in whose theater it would be given, agreed to finance it.

It was a great artistic success, but proved to be a financial disaster which almost cost Diaghilev his company. As it was, he lost the beautiful scenery and costumes by Leon Bakst, which Stoll impounded, and he had to leave England. Furthermore he could not return to the city where he was most likely to recoup his fortunes before he settled the substantial debts.

The Sleeping Princess, as Diaghilev called his new production, introduced to London the young ballerina Olga Spessivtseva (later Spessiva); the role was also danced by Trefilova, Egorova and Lopokova. This ballet also marked the return to the stage of Carlotta Brianza, who had been the original Aurora at the Maryinsky, in the role of Carabosse. This strong sense of continuity is always apparent in ballet history; in fact, it is essential to its progress. Another link with the first production was provided by Enrico Cecchetti, who was now teaching the company. He was the first Bluebird and Carabosse, a role he danced for one last time on his retirement.

This grand production played for over a hundred performances, but that was not enough to make it pay. Sir Oswald Stoll suggested a change of repertoire, but Diaghilev prevaricated and this led Stoll to cancel the production.

The only immediate benefit to Diaghilev, now forced to retreat to Monte Carlo, was that he began to work with Nijinska, who had supervised the production of *The Sleeping Princess*. He entrusted her with his next new production, *Renard*. This was after a generous patron had paid off his debts and he had been able to gather together his company. More importantly he had secured a contract with the Opera House in Monte Carlo to use it as a base in return for performances four months each year.

In 1923 *Renard* was followed by Nijinska's first great work, *Les Noces*. Just as with *The Rite of Spring*, *Les Noces* suggests the impression which the years of touring Russia must have left on the minds of the young Vaslav and Bronislav.

Two more key ballets were to follow in 1924, *The Blue Train* and *Les Biches*. Anton Dolin made his debut in the former, which is not now performed. *Les Biches* was a witty and wicked evocation of the period; as witty and wicked today. It sums up the atmosphere of a house party near a smart beach, with the whole beautifully set in Marie Laurençin's cool décor and costumes.

By now Diaghilev had embarked on a policy which, although imaginative and progressive, lacked cohesion. From his famous comment to Lopokova, 'I am a bartender and have invented certain cocktails,' the period takes its name. Sadly, choreography became the least important ingredient.

The company was still growing and new exciting dancers, who would carry on the great tradition, were joining it. Serge Lifar, who had been a pupil of Nijinska's in Russia, arrived in 1923. He was outstandingly beautiful and created the last great roles of the company before going on to be the single most important figure in French ballet following Diaghilev's death. In 1924 George Balanchine and Alexandra Danilova came from Russia and within a year the first English ballerina arrived. This was the 15-year-old Alice Marks, who changed her name to Markova. Already all the main strands which were to determine the future pattern of ballet were apparent.

Balanchine became choreographer of the company in 1925 and Boris Kochno, Diaghilev's secretary, was influential throughout this period in the preparation of scenarios and supervision of productions.

With few exceptions the ballets from this time are remembered for their avant-garde ideas, their scenario, décor or music, rather than their choreography. Stunning experiments in lighting, what we would call mixed-media events (*Ode*) or décor (the celluloid constructions of Gabo and Pevsner for *La Chatte*) dominated the stage. Only Balanchine produced works which would last, and these, *Apollo* and *The Prodigal Son*, which he produced during the last two years of the company, were so closely entwined with Balanchine's later work that they belong to the story of American ballet.

Above: Deanne Bergsma as the Hostess in the Royal Ballet production of Nijinska's Les Biches, *which retained Marie Laurençin's costumes and decor.*

Above: Mikhail Baryshnikov in Balanchine's The Prodigal Son. *This role has for many years been associated with the outstanding American dancer, Edward Villella.*

Balanchine did, however, play a part in establishing the ballet tradition in England where his other works for the company found favor. His *Romeo and Juliet* had a score by Constant Lambert, *The Gods go a'begging* was danced to Handel tunes arranged by Sir Thomas Beecham, while *The Triumph of Neptune* had a scenario by Sacheverall Sitwell and music by Lord Berners.

Whatever the deficiencies of this period of the Diaghilev Ballet, it was a fertile proving ground for future talent. It also brought into the theater the great painters of the day, which had been the main aim of the Diaghilev-Benois group nearly 40 years before. It provided a stage for the great dancers of the age who might otherwise have been condemned to endless brief appearances in variety, for it must be remembered that there was no similar company in the world at this time. It had also nurtured one of the greatest talents of the ballet in Nijinsky. From his brief period with the company before the Great War, at least seven great ballets still survive.

The efforts of constantly astonishing the public took their toll. When the 1929 summer season in London closed, during which Balanchine had choreographed and Lifar danced *The Prodigal Son*, the company paid a brief visit to Vichy where its last performance took place. The company broke up for its holiday. Diaghilev, after visiting Munich and Salzburg, went to his favorite city, Venice. There, on 19 August 1929, he died.

The Birth of Modern Dance

The history of the classical ballet follows a straight path from court dance to Diaghilev. As an aristocratic art, performed both by and for the upper classes for a great part of its history, it was cocooned from outside pressures and carefully recorded. Only with the advent of Diaghilev did it become truly a 'public' art. In the earliest days of the romantic ballet, patrons at the Paris Opéra were drawn from a limited social group and at its peak in St Petersburg most of the seats were reserved for the Tsar and his court. Commercial pressure and social change widened the audience when Diaghilev first came to Paris. The only other ballet performances available to the general public were individual acts within the framework of a variety bill, some of them of a very high standard.

Modern dance has no such cloistered history and its roots lie in many directions: individual expression, revolt against the establishment, a reaction to the formality of classical ballet. It has become primarily an American art, fitting to a young country with no tradition of classical ballet, a fierce sense of independence and a very considerable ethnic mix.

To define 'modern dance' is not easy. At its simplest it could be said to consist of heightened natural movements expressing a strong theme of real significance, but from this base it is possible to identify almost as many schools of thought as there are performers. They can be loosely grouped into 'schools' but only that of Martha Graham has approached anything comparable to the structure and organization of classical ballet. The modern dance scene is one of constant change, grouping and regrouping, inevitable in view of its intensively personal nature.

Although only one of the very earliest performers was European, many of the first attempts to codify and explain modern or free dance happened in Germany, based on theories from France. Emile-Jacques Dalcroze (1865–1950) and his assistant Rudolf von Laban (1879–1958) were among the first to teach modern dance as a theory, at Dalcroze's school near Dresden.

Dalcroze, who was born in Vienna, was interested in dancing for its use as an aid to music students with a defective sense of rhythm. At his College of Music and Rhythm he expanded the system, called eurythmics, although the emphasis was still heavily theoretical and intellectual.

His assistant Laban was more theatrical, having been influenced by the early performances of Isadora Duncan in Europe. The emphasis was still on dance drama

Right: Mary Wigman

rather than pure dance as a result of his study of the methods expounded earlier in the century by François Delsarte. He was a teacher of acting who wanted to break down the traditional declamatory style used in France in classical drama. His theories even included a list of 10 dramatic passions based on observations of how people actually behave under the stress of emotion. As part of the early cross-fertilization in modern dance, his teaching reached America and had an influence on Isadora Duncan and Ruth St Denis.

Mary Wigman was a pupil of both Dalcroze and Laban and it is through her that the main line of Central European dance developed. She was a better dancer and choreographer than either of her teachers and was to break away from Laban in 1919. The strong intellectual urge of Laban's work was not conducive to great theatrical possibilities and it was natural that he should find common cause with some of Diaghilev's later collaborators, notably the constructivist designers Gabo and Pevsner. Dance was seen as only part of a greater plan and the dancer was little more than a moving part of the décor.

Laban's methods are still strongly advocated and employed in festivals of dance and drama. They have a mathematical quality in their construction which, although uplifting to the participant, offers little to the viewer. These pageants of mass movement allow little place for personal expression except as part of the mass and are probably very reminiscent of the great spectacle Laban mounted for the 1936 Olympics in Berlin. This display was altogether too like the Nazi rallies, which they preferred to keep to themselves, and Laban was forced to leave Germany. He eventually settled in Britain where his methods are used mostly in the educational field.

Mary Wigman showed many of the qualities common to modern dancers of the period and indeed since. She had a very strong personality and a muscular style, almost a deliberate breakaway from the image of the charming ballerina. Her subjects had to have an intrinsic and deep significance and each movement had to express something. Movement for the sake of decoration and attractive stage pictures was quite alien to the cause. It was Hanya Holm, a pupil of Mary Wigman, who carried the messages of Central European dance to America when she opened the Wigman Studio in New York in 1931.

Europe did not provide a particularly fertile home for modern dance, apart from the movement which persisted in Germany, a country with no dance tradition of its own. Even Russia after the Revolution did not take up modern dance in spite of its obvious attractions. If the subjects and their treatment were approved of, the style did not find favor.

Some of the American pioneers, however, did come to Europe to continue their work as, like most innovators, they had not found an audience at home. Isadora Duncan, Ruth St Denis, Maud Allan and Loie Fuller all toured extensively and all had their early great successes in Europe.

Loie Fuller was self-taught, but came from a theatrical family who saw her talents as a dancer from an early age. She toured extensively through France and Germany and was famous for her filmy, floating dresses and the very inventive use of stage lighting. Her technique, like that of Isadora Duncan, who was briefly in her company, was slight, but she more than compensated for this with her flair for production. The image she left behind was, suitably enough, that of stories of beautiful, butterfly-like creatures supporting globes of light. These lamps produced by Tiffany & Company are the epitome of the *art nouveau* period.

Maud Allan was Canadian, but was brought up in America. She had no theatrical background but studied music in Berlin and was deeply influenced by paintings and sculpture. Like Fuller she was self-taught and she was influenced by Isadora Duncan. Although seriously inspired, she is best remembered for an intensely theatrical work, *Vision of Salome*, with its scenes of great passion, scanty clothing and a striking ending when she stroked the severed head of John the Baptist.

Below: Maud Allan

Isadora Duncan

The legend of Isadora has almost eclipsed the work of her contemporaries and to some extent her own. The drama of her life was greater than the dramas she expressed on the stage and these included both the French and Russian Revolutions! Her life story has been popularized on film and television on a scale which suggests some exaggeration, but the bare facts of her career show otherwise. They include passion and intrigue, drama and death, all fuelled by her own, somewhat fanciful, biography *My Life*, which she wrote in the mid-1920s at a time when money was needed. Many inaccuracies can be traced back to this volume, but they are usually mere details of fact and date. The overall picture is exactly right.

Isadora was born in San Francisco in 1878, although this date was often changed in documents to suit herself. Throughout her life she had a cavalier attitude to bureaucracy and the documents it spawns. Little is heard of her father after her birth, but it is clear that her mother was particularly strong-willed. She had to be, as money was scarce. She introduced Isadora and her sister to classical music and it was not long before the talented, and enterprising, girls were giving dancing lessons to the local children to add to the family budget.

When asked when she first danced, Isadora would say, 'In my mother's womb,' but the truth seems less poetic. In later years she said that she had arrived at her

methods without the knowledge of any system, but there is evidence that the teachings of Delsarte (whose book had been published in America in 1885) played some part.

With practically no possessions the family moved to Chicago. Isadora, at this time still just plain Dora but with her knowledge of social dancing, auditioned for a job at the Masonic Roof Garden, which she got. She saw no future in this and eventually moved to New York where she worked for the impresario Daly in a pantomime play starring Jane May. In this she saw neither a future nor any art.

Slightly more prosperous on the proceeds of this engagement, the family decided to move to Britain in 1899. There was no work in prospect. It was only by the lucky chance of Mrs Patrick Campbell seeing her dance in Kensington Palace Gardens that her career got under way. Through Mrs Campbell she met Charles Hallé, son of the founder of the Hallé Orchestra, and through him and other sponsors she eventually gave a recital. She also danced at private parties in the drawing-rooms of rich socialites.

In spite of this success she moved on to Paris, which became her base for the rest of her life. She visited Greece, a source of inspiration, and toured, giving recitals in Vienna where she was seen by an impresario who saw that she could have a wider appeal and arranged for her to visit Budapest. She was a great success in spite of the fact that she was playing to a general audience for the first time, accompanied by an orchestra (she usually danced to a piano). She went on to Berlin where her public success built up so much that she received the sort of acclamation usually reserved for visiting ballerinas.

Bottom left to right: Lynn Seymour in Frederick Ashton's evocation of the Isadora style, Brahms Waltzes.

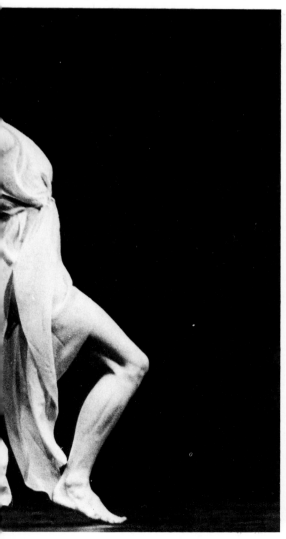

Following the success of these solo performances she decided to form a group and for the next two years toured, including a performance in *Tannhauser* in Bayreuth. In 1904 she went to Russia and appeared in the Hall of the Nobles in St Petersburg. Her performances had a profound effect on Fokine, who at that time was formulating his own ideas in opposition to the Imperial Ballet. Karsavina, too, was influenced. In *Theatre Street* she writes of this visit and how she could not see why the two styles, Isadora and her free dance, and the classical ballet, should not exist side by side and benefit from each other. She also had an influence on Stanislavsky and the dramatic theater.

On her return from Russia she founded a school near Berlin where she had had one of her greatest successes. It was here that she started to conceive her ideas for vast group dances, hundreds of children moving to the music of Beethoven's *Choral Symphony*.

While her dance was continuing to develop, her private life was increasingly complicated. She had children by two lovers, the stage designer Gordon Craig and the millionaire Paris Singer, of the Singer Sewing Machine family. One child died young and the other two were drowned in a terrible accident when their parked car ran into the Seine.

Throughout the war years she continued her school, raising funds for it by endless touring across Europe, America and return visits to Russia. The Russian government invited her to found a school in Moscow in 1921 and her pupils gave performances at the Bolshoi. She married the poet, Sergei Essenine who was twenty years her junior, and left Russia to tour America with him. While there, they were accused of spreading Bolshevism and threatened with expulsion. She returned to Russia where her husband left her before committing suicide. She continued to perform her revolutionary dances, in particular the *Marche Slave* which depicted the struggle of the peasantry. She gave two of her dances at Lenin's funeral, but finally left Russia for Paris.

Here she sold her house and retired to the south of France where she occasionally gave recitals, often sad affairs as she was well into middle age. She died a gruesome death when her long scarf caught in the wheel of a car, killing her instantly.

None of her works survived her. How could they? They were the instinctive reaction of a great artist to the musical works of others. Her technique was limited, her themes simple, but her pioneering message was to be the inspiration for generations of dancers, both modern and classical.

Below: Isadora's impetuous style was brilliantly captured by Vanessa Redgrave in the film Isadora.

The fourth of the founding mothers of American modern dance was Ruth St Denis. She was to become the acknowledged first lady of the American dance. She died only in 1968, a *grande dame* still striking oriental poses at the age of 85.

Miss Ruth, as she became known throughout the dance world, was definitely influenced by the teachings of Delsarte. As a child her mother, who had herself taken lessons from a Delsarte teacher, gave Ruth her first classes. She also attended several dancing schools and by the age of 16 was working in variety as an acrobatic dancer. She even worked for a time in a musical entertainment *The Ballet Girl* and actually danced on point, an episode she later said she was not proud of!

She toured in various musicals, including *Dubarry*, for some years and the lessons she learned about presentation were to prove useful when she produced her own shows. Unusual for modern dancers, especially of this period, she made great use of scenery,

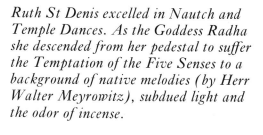

Ruth St Denis excelled in Nautch and Temple Dances. As the Goddess Radha she descended from her pedestal to suffer the Temptation of the Five Senses to a background of native melodies (by Herr Walter Meyrowitz), subdued light and the odor of incense.

lighting effects, and walk-on parts. In fact, in much the same way as Fuller, she created a whole show.

While on tour with *Dubarry* she saw a poster for Egyptian Deities cigarettes and was inspired to create for herself a whole series of dances based on oriental themes. They were not authentic and were more the evocation of a style. Two of the earliest, in 1906, had music by Délibes. Berlin, London and Paris were taken by storm when she toured and Hugo van Hofmannstahl, librettist to Richard Strauss, was a special admirer. She refused all offers to stay in Europe and returned home to work once more in vaudeville.

By 1914 these solos were becoming repetitive and to retain popularity she joined forces with another young modern dancer, Ted Shawn. Together, in 1915, they founded the Denishawn School, which was to be their main achievement.

Shawn had approached dance as a therapy to strengthen his legs following an illness and abandoned his studies for the ministry to become a full-time dancer. He first saw St Denis in 1911 and later convinced her that they would make a perfect partnership. Shawn broke away in the early 1930s to form an all-male company and one of his works *Kinetic Molpai* has recently been revived. In this respect he was unusual, for most of the early modern dance works were dominated by women.

When the Denishawn School ceased operations in 1940, the farm they had used, Jacob's Pillow, became the center of an annual dance festival which still continues. The School was the main training ground for young modern dancers and the most important graduates were Doris Humphrey, Martha Graham, Charles Weidman and Lester Horton. It gave equal emphasis to modern, classical and ethnic dance and in this respect was ahead of its time.

Ted Shawn, extreme left, with his Dance Corporation in their athletic version of Brahms Rhapsody Opus 119.

The new generation of modern dancers took from the old the ideas of freedom and plasticity. What they did not like were the various compromises that had been made. Being in one sense a second generation, but actually the first schooled entirely in the modern movement, their predicament was especially difficult. They did not seek audiences by the effects of lighting and presentation, nor did they lure an audience with evocations of the mysterious east. They were direct and they were uncompromising. Dress was severe and the style even more so.

The only exception to this rule was Lester Horton whose driving passion was a deep and lasting interest in the culture of the American Indian. Naturally this included research about design and costume and his resulting concerts and spectacles laid at least as much emphasis on these as on the dance. He was not a great technician, but had a highly individual style and great sense of character. Following an injury in 1944 he continued to teach and mount his ballets as well as continue his magpie-like collecting urge. He was generous with scholarships and his most famous pupil was Alvin Ailey.

Curiously enough it was the other principal male figure of this era who provided some light relief from the intense works of the women. Charles Weidman could never quite subjugate his fine humorous talents to the cause. He left the Denishawn School to form a company with Doris Humphrey and he proved a perfect foil for her more austere talent.

Humphrey is perhaps one of the most important of this early band as she was more interested in the art of making dances, which became the title of her masterly book, than in performing them. She had started early in modern dance and already had a school before Denishawn was opened. She closed this to study further herself and she

Doris Humphrey, a student of St Denis and Shawn, with her group in New Dance *1936.*

became particularly close to Ruth St Denis, co-creating some works with her, before she left to start a company with Weidman.

She was primarily a creature of intellect and devoted much of her time to expounding the particular theory, briefly referred to as 'fall and recovery,' which was central to her simple and human style. She was forced to stop performing in 1945 and took over the direction of the José Limon company.

Helen Tamiris, the other significant name from this time, unlike Humphrey, did not believe in one firm theory. She had not been at the Denishawn School but had trained at the Metropolitan Opera Ballet. She trod a completely independent path and was not at all doctrinaire. In many ways this gave her more freedom to experiment – she later choreographed *Annie Get Your Gun* – and she was ahead of her contemporaries in other ways. She developed no special technique, but she was among the earliest American dancers to explore their own culture.

Above: Hanya Holm, who is still a force in the teaching of modern dance, with her dancers in Trend. *She also worked in the musical theater and choreographed* Kiss Me Kate *and* My Fair Lady.

Right: Sallie Wilson, Cynthia Gregory (on floor), Bruce Marks and Royes Fernandez in José Limon's The Moor's Pavane, *a retelling of the Othello story.*

Martha Graham

The Denishawn School had its own strong style but it taught a wide range of dance, including ballet (but not on point, according to Martha Graham). The balance was right to allow great individuality and the success of the school can be measured by the number of students who were stimulated to leave and explore their own potential.

Martha Graham was a relatively late starter. Born near Pittsburgh, the family, headed by her doctor father, moved to Santa Barbara when she was 12. Up to this time she had been an expressive child, particularly in the field of dance, but she was only encouraged by the family's Irish maid who had a passion for the theater. At 13 she saw her first professional concert and she resolved to be a dancer, perhaps an indication of the strong will she developed, and needed, in later years. However it was not until she was nearly 20 that she was allowed to attend a summer course at Denishawn – the same year as her father's death, which may have been a decisive factor. Even so she had to finish her formal schooling before she could take up dancing at the school. By 1919 she was a member of the firmly established Denishawn Company and was also teaching at the school. She performed solo dances, such as Ted Shawn's *Xochitl*, but was soon unhappy '. . . at being an attractive young girl on stage in a sari.' She realized very early that she had to have something to dance about. The Denishawn School had a firm belief in dance as a means of communication which Graham could identify with, but she was unsettled with *what* they were communicating.

After she left Denishawn in 1923 she danced two seasons at the Greenwich Village Follies to maintain herself, but at the same time worked as Instructor of Dance at the Eastman School in Rochester. It was here that she began to formulate her own ideas of both technique and subject matter.

Within three years she was establishing her style, but she had not broken completely from the Denishawn mold when in 1926 she gave her first New York recital.

Martha Graham

At this time she was joined by Louis Horst who became her musical director and advisor, as he had been at Denishawn, for well over 20 years. He was an important influence, guiding Graham's musical career through her most creative periods. He also wrote original scores for her, along with many other modern composers, a firm policy of her company from the start.

Her first, historic, recital included many items with ethnic origins, such as *Three Gopi Maidens* and *A Study in Lacquer*, but she established herself firmly as an independent artist and a leading force in the creation of the American modern dance movement.

Her family roots went back to Miles Standish, and her outlook was puritan. Her method was to become completely American, whatever influences might have gone into its making. Her subjects, particularly in these formative years, were drawn from and also added to the American tradition. They were always relevant to the time and expanded the American experience. To progress to American Indian dances from the exotica of Denishawn was part of this growing awareness.

At the same time as her recital debut, Martha Graham opened her studio and seriously began to formulate what we now refer to as the Graham Technique. It was a deliberate and conscious breakaway from the the aerial lightness and search for flight of the classical ballet. She emphasized the relationship with the ground. The bare-foot principle was given a firmer base than the poetic expressions of Isadora. Movement came from the center of the body with a series of contractions and releases. Falls and recoveries emphasized the use of the ground. Group movements were strong and rhythmic, costumes severe and plain. Graham set out to destroy what had gone before by going back to absolute first principles. All easy effect in either dancing or the presentation was stripped away. The dance must speak for itself and it must have something to say.

Martha Graham and her company in Primitive Mysteries.

By 1931 she had created her first lasting masterpiece, *Primitive Mysteries*, which showed her own deep spiritual nature as well as her strong, economical way of expressing it. This theme she pursued throughout her work, transcending creeds, always stressing the universality of the experience.

As a performer she was the center of all her works and had also appeared in 1930 as the Chosen Maiden in Massine's new version of *The Rite of Spring*. Her magnetic stage presence and the total conviction of her movements dominated other performers, but she still gathered around her a company of powerful young dancers – dancers who became very important for the teaching of her technique in the years ahead. The strength of her own performance was one of the few identifiable weaknesses of her choreography; works lost a lot of their impact when danced by another performer. It has taken many difficult years for her company to establish itself, as a company, without her as performer.

In spite of the great sense of struggle during these early years, much of which must have been an inner artistic struggle, Graham achieved a great deal of recognition. Her group was soon making coast-to-coast tours, they danced at the inaugural performance of the Radio City Music Hall and Graham herself was established in academic and government circles.

Perhaps reflecting a social position and her own fierce independence, Graham did not use men in her company until Eric Hawkins joined in 1938. Her subjects, too, had been feminist in outlook. *Frontier* (1935) showed woman as the pioneer with the vast spaces of America ahead of her, a character of strength and determination who reappeared in a later, great work, *Appalachian Spring*.

By 1940 she had taken more men into the company, including Merce Cunningham, and created *Letter to the World*, first shown at Bennington College, Vermont, where she was a teacher. Inspired by, and incorporating, the poetry of Emily Dickinson, this work brilliantly combined word and movement into a whole. It used a Graham technique which appears many times – splitting the role of the central

Left: Appalachian Spring *by Martha Graham, danced to a score which was specially written by Aaron Copland.*

Below: Martha Graham as Mary Queen of Scots, part of her contribution to Episodes, *an evening celebration of Webern's music in collaboration with George Balanchine.*

Bottom right: Martha Graham as Jocasta in Night Journey, *which had sculpted décor by Isamu Noguchi who had worked with her since her earliest performances.*

character. Here there was a central character shown as 'The One who Dances' and 'The One who Speaks'; in *Seraphic Dialogue* there was Joan the Maid, Joan the Warrior and Joan the Saint. Within a year she had started upon one of her most fruitful periods, which produced not only great dances, but the seeds of her magisterial works on mythological themes.

Appalachian Spring is perhaps one of her most perfect creations. It is the story of a young pioneer and his wife taking possession of their new home, simplicity itself, but full of wonder at a new land, and their hopes for the future. Graham's choreography was at one and the same time at its simplest and yet most profound. Aaron Copland produced a radiant score, Noguchi suggested the simple homestead with his usual brilliant economy and Jean Rosenthal lit the whole with a wonderful glow. It is perhaps the summation of all that Graham stood for during her early years.

That same year, 1944, Graham created *Dark Meadow* from which her own writings suggest that her interest in myth and legend grew, an interest heightened by her belief in the collective unconscious.

There followed *Herodiade*, which was more firmly rooted in the classical world (*Dark Meadow* was strongly influenced by Mexican lore), *Cave of the Heart* and *Errand into the Maze*, on the subject of Ariadne and Theseus. The theme of the dance concerns Ariadne and her struggle rather than the heroic tale of Theseus, reflecting Graham's continuing exploration of woman's role. The next great work was *Night Journey*, the story of Jocasta and Oedipus (for we again see the story from Jocasta's point of view) told in psychological terms. These are dances of belief and motivation, not simple retellings of heroic tales, and were brought to the peak of perfection in *Clytemnestra* in 1958.

Throughout this intensely creative period, Graham concentrated much of her thought on the continuing development of her technique. The school was firmly established and the technique codified into a system as firm as that of the classical ballet. Always an innovator and never content to leave things as they are, Graham has continued to refine the technique so that today the eloquent exposition of her style in the film *A Dancer's World* (made in 1956) seems a little too dogmatic. The uncompromising days of her youth, and they had to be uncompromising, are over. The technique is established and can now be used with greater freedom. It is more fluid and flexible. It is essentially more 'dancey' than the heightened dramatic movements of her middle period, when she did in fact maintain a very close contact with the legitimate theater.

The dancers of her company in the 1930s and 1940s – Jane Dudley, Anna Sokolow, Nina Fonaroff, Pearl Lang and many others – have been responsible for the establishment of Graham schools and what are virtually national companies, in Britain and Israel for example, throughout the world. The younger generation of dancers, such as Paul Taylor, are now inventive choreographers in their own right. Others, such as Merce Cunningham, have struck out in a particularly personal way. Just as Denishawn was the major breeding ground for the first wave of talent, so the Graham School was for the second wave.

Martha Graham still choreographs. Her company and school are firmly established. They can no longer rely on her powerful performing personality except as a brilliant speaker, concerned with the wider philosophy of dance. This is now her letter to the world.

Right: The Owl and the Pussycat, *Graham's latest work, with Tim Wengerd as the Owl and Liza Minnelli as the Narrator.*

Europe after Diaghilev

The death of Diaghilev while his company was dispersed vacationing had one advantage. Had he died with the company intact, in rehearsal or during a season, strenuous efforts would probably have taken place to keep the company together. Whatever the personal ambitions of the choreographers, teachers, designers and dancers he had collected around him, there would have been a common desire to keep the company going, as a memorial to his name at least. As it was, with no one person designated as a clear successor – Diaghilev had not been the sort of person to groom one – there was no place for the company to gather and no person for them to rally around.

An attempt to perpetuate the company, which was living on borrowed time anyway, would inevitably have led to eventual demise. Given the personalities involved – Lifar, Balanchine, Stravinsky, Boris Kochno for example – it would have been asking too much of them. We can see some of the problems spelled out if we follow the tangled fortunes of the various Ballets Russes companies, Diaghilev's successors in name only, which managed to tour Europe and America for 15 years after his death.

The Ballet Russe de Monte Carlo and the other companies with similar names and often interchanging personnel did much valuable work in keeping alive interest in the ballet generally while companies such as the Vic-Wells Ballet in Britain were in their infancy. The first company of this name was an amalgam of two ventures started in 1931, that of René Blum based in Monte Carlo and Colonel de Basil, an opera impresario from Paris. Balanchine, Massine and Grigoriev from the Diaghilev company mounted ballets and among the dancers were the new discoveries from the studios of Preobrajenskaya and Kshessinska in Paris – the 'baby' ballerinas, Baronova, Toumanova and Riabouchinska. Massine succeeded Balanchine as ballet master in 1932 when he left to form his own company, Les Ballets 1933. The repertoire included *Petrouchka* and *Prince Igor* as well as *Beau Danube* revived by Massine. He

Leonide Massine in his own ballet, Le Beau Danube, *which is still danced by many companies.*

94

also produced the first of his important 'symphonic' ballets, *Les Presages*, as well as *Jeux d'Enfants*, to show off the talents of the baby ballerinas.

René Blum withdrew from this company and formed his own, which was known as the René Blum Ballet de Monte Carlo, with Fokine as ballet master. Massine joined the company following his disagreements with Colonel de Basil (who by now had a second company headed by Leon Woizikowski) and their fight over the rights to Massine's 'Diaghilev' ballets.

Both companies spent most of their lives touring and were important popularizers of the art of ballet. The rivalry of the companies (which in 1938 gave overlapping seasons in London) and the popularity of the baby ballerinas ensured press interest. The de Basil company eventually became known as the Original Ballet Russe but before its end in 1948 it had not managed to recover from the loss of Massine and many of its dancers such as Danilova and Toumanova.

The Ballet Russe de Monte Carlo (the Blum company) had a more rewarding career artistically and worked extensively in the United States up to 1950. Often referred to as the Denham Ballet Russe after one of its last directors, it finally faded away in the early 1960s. It had given Balanchine a platform and he had created *Night Shadow* and *Danses Concertantes*. It gave a stage to many great dancers who have gone on to influence American Ballet since: dancers such as Krassovska, Youskevitch, Franklin and Danilova.

Denis Nahat, one of the greatest recent performers of the role of the Dancing Master in Massine's Gaîté Parisienne, *created for the Ballet Russe de Monte Carlo in 1938.*

While Diaghilev was alive there was only one other major company, which performed much the same function as the various Ballets Russes in popularizing ballet. Anna Pavlova arranged her company as a vehicle for her own talents. The artistic policy was conservative and traditional but without any particular respect for tradition as far as the classics were concerned. She cut them to suit herself and only her own great creative gifts and glowing talent can be used as an excuse for this.

She had begun touring as early as 1907 when she joined a group of dancers from the Imperial Theater organized by Adolph Bolm. They played in major theaters throughout northern Europe, giving well-received performances in Copenhagen and Stockholm. During the holiday the following year, Pavlova and Bolm decided to tour again, adding Berlin and Prague to their itinerary and shortened versions of *La Fille Mal Gardée, Giselle* and *Swan Lake* to their repertoire.

As with *Coppelia* and *Paquita* these were ballets Pavlova was well-known in at the Maryinsky and she did not get any more adventurous as time went on. Fokine had created *The Dying Swan* for her and she had inspired him in *Les Sylphides*, but she did not work successfully with him again as his ballets were not good vehicles for her individual performance.

Pavlova joined Diaghilev for the first Paris season of his Ballet Russe, but almost inevitably their future was not to be together. Pavlova was an established prima ballerina and was not open to the new style in the same way as Karsavina.

After this Paris season she toured once again, this time with Mikhail Mordkin as her partner, and appeared in London at the Palace Theater in 1910. She danced with great success as part of a variety bill, so great that she arranged a further visit that same year with a larger company and presented *La Fille Mal Gardée* in place of the usual series of divertissements.

This marked the start of Pavlova's pioneering work for the ballet. In 1911 she went to America for the first of many extensive tours (she saw the young Martha Graham dance at the Greenwich Follies just 12 years later) and it was on this trip that she parted from Mordkin to become sole star, director, organizer and inspiration.

For Diaghilev's first London season Pavlova rejoined his company and London became her home from that time. In 1912 she bought Ivy House in North London and in 1913 took up permanent residence following her resignation from the Imperial Theaters. The house is now the Pavlova Museum. That same year she embarked on her most ambitious tour of America, taking, for the first time, a full company and complete sets and costumes for full-length ballets. Up to her death in The Hague in 1931 she kept this organization on the move, giving mostly one night stands in major cities as well as throughout the provinces of Britain, the backwoods towns of America, across Australia and New Zealand and even on to Japan.

As with so many other dancers, the Great War cut Pavlova off from Russia, a break made permanent by the Revolution of 1917. In spite of her resignation from the Maryinsky she was invited back to dance for the Tsar, but she never returned. In Britain she found not only a home but also an adoring public and more importantly the raw material for her company. English girls proved to be the perfect quiet type for her to dominate and shape as her *corps de ballet*. They must also have had remarkable stamina to manage the touring schedule she arranged. These same girls and the ballet schools which trained them were to be an important factor in the later renaissance and growth of British ballet.

Ballet in Britain was deliberately developed along carefully planned lines with a firm aim in mind. The opportunities presented by the dissolution of the Diaghilev company were grasped and his dancers and ballet masters were assimilated into British ballet life. Other countries in Europe either had no chance to benefit or did not do so even though the opportunity was there.

Certain countries such as Denmark and Sweden had a strong ballet tradition of their own, though the Swedish one was going through particularly barren times. Before Diaghilev's death the Royal Danish Ballet had invited Fokine to work with them and

Below : The politicians make empty gestures in Kurt Jooss's The Green Table.

they had taken to the ballets well. Fortunately they did not allow this to displace their own precious tradition and after Fokine's departure they continued to go their own way. They based their repertoire firmly on the Bournonville classics for which we are all grateful today. At the time they guarded them jealously, perhaps too jealously, as it was not until the late 1940s that companies outside Denmark actively helped to produce Bournonville works.

Though Fokine did good work in 1925 (and authentic versions of his ballets, particularly *Petrouchka*, have been carefully preserved there), it was a young dancer, Harald Lander, who took up the traditions of Bournonville through his teacher, the former ballet master, Hans Beck. Beck was in a direct line from Bournonville, who had died only a few days after Beck's debut at the theater, and produced many of the important ballets from his master's repertoire. Essentially these are the versions we have today.

Lander and his contemporaries, such as Hans Brenaa and Niels Bjorn Larsen (both active today in carrying on the tradition), revitalized the tradition, building upon the firm base of the Royal Danish Ballet School which, rather unusually, had a tradition of producing fine male dancers. It is still looked to for male dancers rather than ballerinas which can only arise from the fact that after *La Sylphide* Bournonville was first concerned with producing dances for himself, or dancers in his mold. Lander guided the fortunes of the company up to 1951 when he left to join the Paris Opéra from where the Danish tradition of romantic dancing had originally come.

In spite of a very illustrious past in the days of Gustav III at the end of the eighteenth century, by the 1930s there was no serious ballet in Sweden. Fokine had visited Stockholm immediately after leaving Diaghilev in 1913 and among others he encouraged was the ballerina Carina Ari whose name is perpetuated by a major national award for the dance.

Most of the potential talent of the Royal Swedish Ballet who could have carried on the tradition did not return to Sweden after the breakup of the Ballets Suédois, which Rolf de Mare had organized in Paris in 1920 – the only company which made any attempt to rival Diaghilev. Together with the choreographer Jean Borlin and the dancers he had taken from Sweden, de Mare concocted cocktails as exotic as those of the master. Auric, Poulenc and Milhaud, together with Fernand Leger and George de Chirico, collaborated with them to produce such ballets as *La Création du Monde*, *Les Mariés de la Tour Eiffel* and *Maison de Fous*.

In spite of a gifted ballet mistress, Lisa Steier, who stayed in Stockholm, little of importance happened there in the field of classical ballet. Expressionist dance did find one major exponent, Birgit Akesson, who inspired a later generation of choreographers after the war, including Birgit Cullberg.

In Germany, too, it was expressionist dance which rose to prominence. In spite of having enthusiastically welcomed Pavlova and then Diaghilev on their first tours it did not develop a tradition of its own. The many small courts had troupes of dancers, but as a general rule their position was subservient to the opera. It was not until after the 1940 war that a classical tradition took root and even then it was some years before it flowered.

By the 1930s Mary Wigman was well established as performer and teacher and Kurt Jooss, a pupil of both Sigurd Leeder and Laban, started his first groups. After an initial attempt in Münster in 1924, the group moved to Essen in 1927 and was soon made the official company by the two theaters there. Although, like many creative artists, Jooss was forced to leave soon after the rise of the Nazis, he did eventually return there in the 1950s. His key work, *The Green Table*, which satirized the feeble attempts of politicians at the Peace Conference, was created in England where he found a home at Dartington Hall. Before leaving Germany, however, he was inspired to produce his own versions of some Diaghilev masterpieces, including *Petrouchka* and *The Prodigal Son*, soon after Diaghilev's death.

Above: **The Big City,** *created by Jooss in the same year as* **The Green Table,** *shows the evils of city life in a style closely associated with the works of Brecht and Weill.*

During this period there was little classical ballet activity in either Belgium, once the base of Jean Antoine Petipa (father of both Lucien and Marius), or Holland. For a real revival Belgium had to wait until another French choreographer came to Brussels in 1959. This was Maurice Bejart. Holland had one foot on the road to modern dance with the activities of Yvonne Georgi and soon after the war the Scapino Ballet was founded. Since that time a thriving joint tradition has been established.

Unlike these countries Italy had had a glorious tradition, but by 1930 it was artistically bankrupt. However the schools, particularly in Milan, continued to produce good dancers just as they had done in the great days of the classical ballet in Russia.

The great teacher, Cecchetti, returned in 1925, but was too old to achieve much and apart from efforts by Aurol Milloss at the Rome Opera House during the war, ballet lay fallow there for many years. Its great tradition has gone, but it provides a fitting resting place, in Venice, for both Diaghilev and Stravinsky.

As both Paris and Monte Carlo had provided a haven for Diaghilev, it would have seemed the most natural thing for France to be the main beneficiary of his legacy, rather than Britain. However the strains which George Balanchine noticed when he was invited to work at the Paris Opéra were to inhibit any wide progress there.

During Diaghilev's lifetime the Ballets Russes had had an effect on the Paris Opéra and the then director, Rouché, invited many of Diaghilev's discoveries and collaborators to work there. Stravinsky, Ibert and Dukas composed; Dufy and Bakst designed; Fokine choreographed. Pavlova and Spessivtseva performed as guests, while Carlotta Zambelli reigned as the resident star.

Following Balanchine's illness and subsequent withdrawal from the Opéra, Serge Lifar took over the choreography for *The Creatures of Prometheus* and then the position of ballet master. He remained at the Opéra for 25 years and became an institution in France. French soldiers would even refer to their long underwear as *sergelifars*.

The last of Diaghilev's close friends, Lifar was a particularly handsome and striking dancer and developed as a choreographer. In both capacities he dominated the Opéra. Under his direction the Opéra School produced a new generation of ballerinas including Yvette Chauviré and Lycette Darsonval, and by wartime there was a flowering of talent which came to full bloom when hostilities ended.

Of course it must be remembered that there was much activity in France with the various Ballets Russes companies of Blum and de Basil, but these are not really part of the renewal of French tradition. Constantly on tour, they belong to the story of ballet as a whole and their influence can be found in major national companies or small towns where dancers stayed behind to found schools and local companies.

Roland Petit was a product of the Paris Opéra School and a very precocious student. By 1940 he was in the *corps de ballet* and within a year was working on independent projects with Janine Charrat. By 1944 this had grown into the Ballet du Champs Elysées which had much in common with the later Diaghilev period, including his associates, Cocteau, Bérard and Boris Kochno.

Petit produced many works for this company, including *Jeune Homme et la Mort* for the spectacular male dancer Jean Babilée, before he left to form another company Ballet de Paris with which Margot Fonteyn made one of her few overseas guest appearances in the 1940s. It also provided brilliant vehicles for dancers such as Zizi Jeanmaire (Carmen in 1949) who married Petit, and Violette Verdy. The latter went on to become the least typical, but one of the most charming and musical, ballerinas of Mr Balanchine in New York and then returned to direct the Opéra for two seasons from 1978.

Right: Kirsten Simone and Erik Bruhn of the Royal Danish Ballet in their production of Roland Petit's Carmen, roles originally danced by Zizi Jeanmaire and Petit himself.

While Europe and America were in differing ways reaping the benefit of the Diaghilev experience, Russia was plowing a separate furrow after being cut off from the main stream of ballet and dance by the Revolution. Most of the dance talent of Russia had chosen exile with Diaghilev, been forcibly cut off in 1917, or had decided to leave later. Few returned to work there, a major and significant exception being the composer Prokofiev who had worked with Diaghilev on several ballets including *The Prodigal Son*. He was not welcomed back with open arms and had to face increasing criticism for his lack of social realism before making his many major contributions to Soviet ballet.

The Revolution had been a major blow to the art of classical ballet in Russia. Whatever the artistic considerations, the fact remained that it had been part of the Tsar's court and as such there were demands for it to be destroyed along with the other trappings of a tyrannical monarchy.

The Maryinsky Theater changed its name to the State Academy of Opera and Ballet (later, in 1934, being called the Kirov in memory of an assassinated Soviet leader) and the school reopened. The *corps de ballet* was still largely intact, but it was some time before the company grew. That it did is largely a tribute to the teaching tradition and, in particular, the efforts of Agrippina Vaganova. It was also fortunate that the Commissar for Public Education was both a close friend of Lenin and a keen follower of the ballet. His political point was that the people should inherit the glories of the court and not destroy them, in much the same way as they would inherit the farms and the factories.

It would have seemed more natural, given the nature of the Revolution, for modern dance to have had an appeal, but the visits of Isadora Duncan, at the invitation of the government, and home-grown efforts came to nothing. Some elements within Russia persisted and even suggested that Diaghilev should return, for at this time he was going through his cocktail period and attempting expressionist ballets which they thought would suit socially realistic themes.

Below left: The Red Flower, *a reworking of* The Red Poppy, *with Struchkova and Lapauri at the Bolshoi.*

Below right: Vakhtang Chaboukiani.

It was the Vaganova teaching method which eventually took root and the products of her school became the generation of great Russian dancers which established the peculiar 'Russian' style we speak of today – the big movements, the spectacular jumps, the expressive use of arms and flexible backs. It is a style full of athleticism, softened into art.

During the late 1920s and 1930s it was the subject matter of ballets which had to live up to the revolutionary ideal: ballets such as *The Red Poppy* (Russian Sailors helping Chinese peasants) and *The Flames of Paris* (the French Revolution). By the time of *The Fountain of Bakchisarai* in 1934 the trend was slowly moving away from social realism, although not without problems, and works such as *Gayaneh* (love on a collective farm) continued to be produced.

Even Prokofiev's monumental *Romeo and Juliet* had a difficult birth. Perhaps as a result of Prokofiev being generally out of favor, the first time the score was used was in Brno in 1938, but it eventually reached the stage of the Kirov Theater in 1940. Galina Ulanova danced the role of Juliet with Sergeyev as Romeo. It was later staged in the Bolshoi Theater, Moscow and it is this monumental production which has been preserved on film. The choreography by Lavrovsky is uneven and reflects a return to the Petipa-like construction of ballet, but Ulanova's artistry blended the various styles of dance into a cohesive whole.

Galina Ulanova became prima ballerina assoluta, the first complete product of the Vaganova system and the first truly Soviet ballerina. Curiously enough she tempered the athletic Russian style with acute sensibility and a perfect, unforced technique. If she was the epitome of the Soviet ballerina, Vakhtang Chaboukiani was to be the model for a generation of male dancers. He elevated technique to new levels and created a host of roles which gave a whole new repertoire to the male dancer.

The dispersal of dancers from the main centers during the war was responsible for a remarkably high standard of dancing throughout the multitude of regional companies in Russia. It is from these schools that the Bolshoi and the Kirov are now finding their new young dancers.

Top left: Galina Ulanova in the film of the Bolshoi Romeo and Juliet.

Top right: Ekaterina Maximova and Vladimir Vasiliev in Romeo and Juliet.

Ballet in Britain

By the turn of the century ballet in Britain was very much part of the variety theater, but the standard of dancing and presentation was high and it was immensely popular. Great dancers appearing alongside the big names of the music hall introduced ballet to a very wide public which was only good for the growth of ballet. If it had been an élite art, as was the ballet in Paris for instance, it may never have developed as it did.

At the Empire and Alhambra, ballet dominated the programs. Commercial managements may have been intent on dazzling their public with gorgeous décor, pretty girls and an outstanding ballerina, but such was the talent of dancers like Adeline Genée, Lydia Kyasht and Phyllis Bedells that they ended up with a performance worthy of an opera house.

In general, managements preferred specially created ballets, usually without a balletic background, but Adeline Genée, the great Danish ballerina, persuaded the management of the Empire to mount *Coppelia* in 1906. It proved a triumph and undoubtedly played a great part in the re-establishment of ballet as an independent art. This success, like many others, has been a little overshadowed by the impact of Diaghilev's enterprise. Music Hall ballet ended, but in its place the British national ballet grew. Adeline Genée continued her great dancing career with considerable success in America and Britain and became an important and influential force in the establishment of the Royal Academy of Dancing.

Below left to right: Lydia Kyasht, Adeline Genée and Phyllis Bedells.

Soon after working with Nijinsky on *The Rite of Spring* and the fateful South American tour when he married Romola Pulsky, Marie Rambert came to London in 1914. The daughter of a bookseller in Warsaw, she followed in Isadora's footsteps and then trained with Dalcroze, which led to her joining forces with Diaghilev. Although employed for her knowledge of modern technique and its use in unravelling the complex rhythms of *The Rite of Spring*, she became interested in the classical ballet largely through the inspiration of Karsavina. Once in London she began to take lessons from the great teachers Cecchetti and Serafina Astafieva, who had also taught Alicia Markova and Anton Dolin.

While studying herself she opened her own school in Notting Hill Gate, London, supported by her husband, the playwright Ashley Dukes. One of her early pupils was Frederick Ashton, a young man who had been inspired to dance by Pavlova in Lima, Peru. He had already studied in London with Massine in the early 1920s before meeting Rambert, who fostered his choreographic talent.

At this time there were two parallel strands in the development of ballet in Britain which within a decade had intertwined to produce the Vic-Wells ballet – destined to become the Royal Ballet – and the Ballet Rambert.

While Ashton was working with Rambert and already beginning to choreograph,

Right: Alexander Grant and Merle Park in Frederick Ashton's A Wedding Bouquet, *which is accompanied by Lord Berners' fashionable music and Gertrude Stein's verses.*

Ninette de Valois was opening her school in London. She, too, had worked with Diaghilev as a dancer, after a career in London as principal dancer with Sir Thomas Beecham's Opera Company and the groups organized in the early twenties by Massine and Lopokova. De Valois had already determined to form her own company, but with brilliant foresight saw that it must be firmly based on a school, her Academy of Choreographic Art. That same year she met Lilian Baylis of the Old Vic Theatre and arranged to stage the dances for the productions there. This was the start of a close working relationship which extended to the Sadler's Wells Theatre and eventually led to the formation of the Royal Ballet.

1930 saw the formation of two important groups: the Ballet Club, centered on Rambert's activities, and the Camargo Society. This was wider based, with an educational slant, and its leaders had already been instrumental in arranging ballet performances by visiting artists such as Karsavina, Mary Wigman, Markova and Dolin throughout the 1920s. They gave performances in West End theaters and presented important new works such as *Façade* by Ashton and *Job* by de Valois, as well as revivals of the classics which would in later years become the firm basis of the repertoire of the growing national ballet. Painters such as Augustus John, Edmund Burra and Edmond Dulac designed ballets and important composers such as William Walton and Ralph Vaughan Williams contributed music.

Marie Rambert's performances were based in the tiny Mercury Theatre which also housed the ballet school. Frederick Ashton's first ballet, *A Tragedy of Fashion*, was presented in 1926 as part of the revue *Riverside Nights*, and he went on to choreograph for both Rambert and de Valois until he became resident choreographer of the Vic-Wells Ballet in 1935.

At the Mercury Theatre, in spite of its tiny stage, which is given a brief moment of glory in the film *The Red Shoes* when Moira Shearer danced *Swan Lake*, Rambert also mounted productions of the classics and the dancers included Markova, Karsavina, Woizikowski, and, later, both Robert Helpmann and Margot Fonteyn.

Above: Fernando Bujones in the American Ballet Theater production of Les Patineurs *for an American television special.*

The Vic-Wells Ballet came into being in 1931 with the establishment, by de Valois and Lilian Baylis, of a joint company to serve both the Old Vic and Sadler's Wells, to which it eventually moved. It inherited the resources of the Camargo Society when the latter ceased operations in 1933, by which time it was already well on the way to becoming an established ballet company.

Alicia Markova gave the young company her support and was ballerina from 1932 to 1935. She was succeeded by the young Margot Fonteyn, and the company attracted Pearl Argyle and Harold Turner from the Rambert Company as well as a young Australian, Robert Helpmann. Constant Lambert became musical director and was to be a great influence on British ballet until his death.

During its earliest years the Vic-Wells Ballet, with de Valois at its head, pursued a policy of mounting original works and the classics. Ninette de Valois created *Checkmate* and *The Rake's Progress*, while Ashton, with Fonteyn as a source of inspiration, produced *Les Rendezvous*, *Les Patineurs*, *Nocturne* and *Apparitions*.

Something of the strength of the ballet during this period can be seen from the immense public attracted by all these groups. The visits of the Ballets Russes had shown that there was a large popular following for ballet.

When Markova left the Vic-Wells Ballet she joined forces with Anton Dolin to form a large-scale touring company, the first of several ventures together which eventually became the London Festival Ballet. Sadly the first effort, though well financed, was not a great artistic success and concentrated on the classics with only a handful of minor new works. Even so they did attempt a 12-week London season in 1936, but their greatest successes took place outside London, bringing ballet to new audiences.

Below: Ninette de Valois allegory about love, Checkmate, *with its period décor by the artist, E. McKnight Kauffer.*

While de Valois was concentrating on what seems, in retrospect, a very clear line of thought and action to create a national company, Marie Rambert continued to produce not only good dancers but, most importantly, a whole generation of choreographers. She had an eye for choreographic talent and the knowledge to encourage it. Many left Rambert, often for purely financial reasons as she could offer only the lowest expenses, but some joined her own permanent company. After Ashton's departure, though he had never belonged in the strict sense of the word, Rambert encouraged Walter Gore, Andrée Howard and Anthony Tudor.

Tudor had joined Rambert as a late-starting student in 1928 at the age of 19. Rambert immediately took him under her wing and provided odd jobs around the theater to keep him, as well as encouraging him to choreograph. Just over two years later he produced his first work, *Cross Gartered*, based on Elizabethan dances.

In many ways Tudor was to create a new classical style which mirrored many of the developments of the modern dance movement. He was interested in the psychological implications of human relationships and in communicating them through the use of the classical technique. His second ballet, *Lysistrata*, followed soon after and was particularly well-constructed. He went on to produce works which are modern

classics, works such as *Lilac Garden* and *Dark Elegies*. His total output was small, but the effect was very influential and proved important to the development of American ballet following the Second World War.

Following difficulties during the production of *Dark Elegies*, unquestionably a work of genius, Tudor left Rambert in 1938 and formed his own company, the London Ballet. Business problems and the day-to-day running of the company limited his output during this period, but he produced one of the great satirical comedy ballets, *Judgement of Paris*. For his London Ballet he planned a dramatic work, *Pillar of Fire*, but never-ending financial problems forced the closure of the company and Tudor, together with Hugh Laing, a talented dancer and designer, accepted an invitation to join American Ballet Theater.

The years before the war were busy for British ballet. Ballet Rambert, with some of the dancers returning from the Tudor company, continued to tour while the Vic-Wells Ballet with Fonteyn and Helpmann established as its stars approached its most ambitious program to date.

In 1939 de Valois, using the invaluable notebooks brought from Russia by Sergeyev, produced *The Sleeping Beauty*, with Margot Fonteyn as Aurora.

Far left: Anthony Tudor rehearsing.

Left: Antoinette Sibley and Anthony Dowell as the ill-fated lovers in Tudor's Lilac Garden.

Right: Joan Cadzow as La Dessée de la Danse in Tudor's Gala Performance, *which wittily exaggerates the dance styles of Russia, France and Italy.*

Margot Fonteyn

Margot Fonteyn remembers a photograph of Adeline Genée, demonstrating the positions of the arms, on the wall of her teacher's studio in the London suburb of Ealing. She followed Dame Adeline as President of the Royal Academy of Dancing 40 years later. Like so many other dancers her first contact with ballet, as opposed to the children's dancing Miss Bosustow taught, was when she saw a poster advertising Anna Pavlova. Little Miss Hookham, as she then was, decided that if Pavlova was the greatest dancer in the world, as her mother told her, she would be the second greatest. Unfortunately, apart from her mother's comparison of their respective *retirés*, she has no recollection of the world's greatest dancer.

She made her own stage debut at the age of four, as a 'Wind' in a babies' ballet, with her brother Felix featuring as the principal dancer. However, the first important stage in her ballet education happened a long way from Ealing. Her father, an engineer, was appointed to a post in Shanghai and it was here that she took serious lessons with a Russian emigré, Madame Takaranova, and, more importantly, met the Russian George Gontcharov. He had started teaching and had founded a trio to perform in night clubs with George Toropov and Vera Volkova. Both Gontcharov and Volkova became important in the British ballet scene and Volkova took her Russian teaching to the Royal Danish Ballet in Copenhagen.

On the family's return to England Fonteyn took classes with Serafina Astafieva, whose star pupil, Markova, had joined Diaghilev at the age of 14. Soon, however, her mother wanted to move her to the Vic-Wells School with the absolute certainty that if young Margot wanted to make a career in ballet that was the place to be. Here she met with the approval of Ninette de Valois who thought she had arrived just in time 'to save her feet' (later described by Ashton as 'little pats of butter').

It was not long before she took her place in the *corps de ballet*, while still a student, as a Snowflake in *The Nutcracker*, and soon after she took her first principal part in an Ashton ballet, *Rio Grande*. At precisely what point Fonteyn's professional career started she is not sure. At one moment she was a student and doing tiny roles, at another a solo part. She can only remember that in 1935, a year after her audition for the school, Ninette de Valois told her one evening after a performance of *Les Sylphides* that she need not wear the regulation student dress any more.

From the start she liked, and therefore excelled at, the lyrical roles and throughout her career she has captured audiences by her musical qualities and not by sheer technique. At about this same time she found her two special partners, Michael Somes and Robert Helpmann.

It was also this year that Markova left the Vic-Wells Ballet, leaving Fonteyn as the heir apparent. De Valois had the future mapped out. She had two good male dancers, she had Ashton as choreographer and she had Fonteyn. Until Fonteyn officially took over as prima ballerina the company used Pearl Argyle, who was exceptionally beautiful, with other roles shared out between Mary Honer, Elizabeth Miller, Pamela May, June Brae and Fonteyn.

Fonteyn, however, had a special appeal to Ashton and he soon created *Le Baiser de la Fée* for her. She also danced, in 1935, her first Odette in *Swan Lake*, sharing the role with Ruth French as Odile. Other roles followed in profusion, mostly created by Ashton, until 1939 when *The Sleeping Beauty* was proposed. It was finally produced under the Diaghilev title *The Sleeping Princess*, much to Fonteyn's relief as she did not think she lived up to the title 'Beauty'. At first she found the characterization elusive, but it became her key role.

While on tour in Liverpool war was declared and the whole company was stranded in Holland during the period of the phony war in early 1940, a period which inspired Ashton to create *Dante Sonata* using a modern dance idiom. Throughout the war

Fonteyn appeared constantly with the ballet, which proved invaluable entertainment both on tour and in London.

The Sadler's Wells Ballet, with Fonteyn at its head, moved to the Royal Opera House in 1946 and *The Sleeping Beauty* was chosen to open the first season in a sumptuous new production designed by Oliver Messel. The success of this evening was echoed three years later when in the same ballet Fonteyn made such a great impact in America at the Metropolitan Opera House.

With Ashton out of the armed forces a further period of creativity followed, the jewel of which was, and indeed remains, *Symphonic Variations*. It was Ashton's first abstract or, at least, plotless ballet and was designed by Sophie Fedorovitch. Massine, too, arrived in London and mounted *The Three Cornered Hat* for Fonteyn while Ashton's *Cinderella* was on the horizon.

During these years as the prima ballerina of the Royal Ballet, Fonteyn made few forays into the outside world, the only significant one being her guest appearance with Roland Petit's company in Paris where she danced the role cf Agathe, the white cat, in *Demoiselles de la Nuit*.

In 1948 a small injury during the first performance of Ashton's *Don Juan* made Fonteyn conscious of her position as head of a company which then included such brilliant young ballerinas as Beryl Grey, Violetta Elvin and Moira Shearer. Although not yet 30 she admitted to uncertainty and indeed a great degree of jealousy when it was announced that she would dance *Cinderella* alternating with Shearer. Up to that point she had had Ashton all to herself. As it was, the injury cost her more than one performance and Shearer had great success in the role. By that time Shearer had also made an international name through her film *The Red Shoes*, which remains to this day one of the best ballet films.

Far left: Margot Fonteyn in the Shadow Dance from Ashton's Ondine.

Left: Fonteyn as Aurora.

Fonteyn continued to head the Royal Ballet up to 1959 and added two more great Ashton works to her repertoire: *Daphnis and Chloe* and *Ondine*. *Ondine* is the summation of the relationship between Ashton and Fonteyn. He created for her a masterpiece which used every ounce of her talent and personality. It has been described as 'a concerto for Fonteyn,' a concerto for a unique instrument. At the age of 40 her career seemed to be reaching a peak but instead it reached new heights and went on for another 20 years.

While dancing in Russia Fonteyn heard from home that a young Russian dancer had defected to the West from the Leningrad Kirov Ballet which had been on tour in Paris. He was reported to be their best young dancer. Indeed he was. It was Rudolf Nureyev.

Little realizing the importance it would have for her own career, which she firmly thought was on the downward path, Fonteyn invited Nureyev to dance at one of the galas she arranged for the Royal Academy of Dancing. She found him through Vera Volkova in Copenhagen where he was working. It appeared he was keen to dance with her but initially she did not share his enthusiasm. As it turned out, because of Fonteyn's diffidence, Nureyev first appeared in London dancing a specially created solo by Ashton and the *Swan Lake pas de deux* with Rosella Hightower.

Ninette de Valois engaged Nureyev to dance *Giselle* at Covent Garden and asked Fonteyn to dance with him. Her immediate reaction, in her own words, was to say that '. . . it would be like mutton dancing with lamb' but instead she decided to do the performance on the grounds that if Nureyev was to be the sensation of the season she might just as well get on the bandwagon!

And so started a partnership perhaps unique in ballet history. Their joint names became synonymous with ballet to vast audiences through television or gossip column. They created great works together, such as Ashton's *Marguerite and Armand* and gave performances of the classics, in particular *Giselle*, which surpassed earlier achievements. Inevitably a great deal of their time was spent dancing various *pas de deux* in endless gala tours, but Fonteyn's artistry never deserted her and she continues to perform, amazing as it may seem, at the age of 60.

Above: Fonteyn in Ashton's **Cinderella** *with Ashton and Helpmann as the Ugly Sisters.*

Right: Fonteyn and Nureyev in Ashton's **Marguerite and Armand,** *an emotional reworking of* **The Lady of the Camellias.**

Ballet in America

During the nineteenth century ballet in America invariably meant a tour by one of the great ballerinas of the age. Americans saw a production of *La Sylphide* as early as 1835 and *Giselle* in 1846. Fanny Elssler toured triumphantly in 1840 and Carlotta Brianza danced in 1883. Anna Pavlova, who danced practically everywhere possible, had much the same effect in America as in England and inspired a generation of dance students and audiences alike. With the arrival of the Diaghilev company in 1916 and 1917 interest in Russian Ballet was aroused, but there was little native activity of note.

It was following the death of Diaghilev that ballet in America began to come alive. In 1933 the Ballet Russe de Monte Carlo (de Basil) made the first of many appearances and in 1934 George Balanchine went to America to direct the School of American Ballet. The arrival of a product of the Imperial Theater of St Petersburg marks the birth of all-American ballet.

Below: Alexandra Danilova and Frederick Franklin in Danses Concertantes, *which George Balanchine created for the Ballet Russe de Monte Carlo in 1944.*

George Balanchine

At the age of ten, in 1914, George Balanchine joined the Imperial School, having already studied music from an early age. He graduated with honors in 1921 and joined the *corps de ballet* of the post-Revolutionary company. At the same time he continued his music studies at the Petrograd (soon to become Leningrad) Conservatory. This musical background has been a great influence in his choreography and if there are slight differences of opinion about the musicality of some of his ballets, his understanding of music is undisputed. It seems almost inevitable that he should have found a natural ally and friend in Igor Stravinsky when he joined the Diaghilev company.

While in Petrograd Balanchine fell foul of the theater authorities when he arranged two evenings of experimental ballet. It seems odd in retrospect that he offended the people who were trying to preserve the old tradition rather than the revolutionaries. Balanchine left Russia in 1924 as part of a small group known as the Soviet State Dancers, which included Tamara Geva and Alexandra Danilova. They left with their belongings literally tied up in brown paper. They knew that they would not return.

They arrived in Berlin and fortunately were able to arrange first of all a tour of the Rhineland and then an engagement at the Empire Theatre in London. They were not a great success as they knew nothing about the slick style of presentation needed on a variety bill, but they did attract the notice of Diaghilev.

Below: Monica Mason, Svetlana Beriosova and Georgina Parkinson, with Donald Macleary in the Royal Ballet production of Balanchine's Apollo.

Balanchine had not heard much of Diaghilev in Russia and of his first meeting could only remember '. . . an impressive looking gentleman with a perfume or hair tonic that was scented with almonds.' Danilova even took offence at being asked to audition for him. As a test piece Balanchine mounted his *Funeral March* for some of the dancers, including Ninette de Valois. Diaghilev approved. Balanchine was appointed ballet master of this major company at the age of 20.

Balanchine's career with Diaghilev is well documented. Before the dissolution of the company he had provided works of sufficient notoriety to satisfy the needs of Diaghilev's fickle public. He had also created two lasting masterpieces, *Apollon Musagète* (now called *Apollo*) and *The Prodigal Son*.

Within a few weeks of Diaghilev's death, Balanchine was invited to stage Beethoven's *The Creatures of Prometheus* at the Paris Opéra and was offered the post of ballet master. Balanchine was tempted by the offer, but was well aware of the politics and intrigue which surrounded the theater, as well as the prevailing artistic attitude. As things turned out, he did not have to make a decision. Before starting on *The Creatures of Prometheus* in the studio, but with the basic plan well worked out, Balanchine contracted pneumonia and handed the production over to Serge Lifar. Initially diffident, Lifar became self-confident and was soon well-established at the Opéra himself.

Balanchine was then offered work by Charles B. Cochran who was planning his new revue for 1930. In about eight weeks' rehearsal time Balanchine not only created three ballets and a finale, but also acquired a taste for working in the musical theater. Already as he was preparing this revue the first ideas of working in America were being put to him.

John Martin, the eminent American critic saw the revue and wrote appreciatively about the ballets. In an interview with him, Balanchine said that he was sure he would work in the United States before the year was out. In fact he spent the rest of the year as guest ballet master with the Royal Danish Ballet in Copenhagen where he staged works from the Diaghilev repertoire, including *Scheherazade, La Boutique Fantasque* and his own *Apollo*. He returned to England to work once more in variety, this time for Sir Oswald Stoll at the Coliseum presenting '16 Delightful Balanchine Girls 16' as the posters proclaimed.

The newly formed Ballet Russe de Monte Carlo (Blum/de Basil) invited Balanchine to join the venture as ballet master, and for them he not only discovered the 'baby' ballerinas, having told the 27-year-old Danilova that she was too old, but mounted ballets such as *Cotillon*. This relationship was not to last as Balanchine did not get on with de Basil, whom he called a crooked octopus, and he left to form a small group of his own. Les Ballets 1933 started with little capital but a firm modernistic policy. There was deliberately no mention of Russian ballet in the title.

The company gave a glittering season at the Champs Elysées Theater in Paris in direct competition to the Ballet Russe de Monte Carlo (de Basil) at the Chatelet.

In spite of the array of talent Balanchine had gathered around him – Tilly Losch, Pearl Argyle, Derain, Berard, Brecht, Weill and Milhaud – the public flocked to the Ballet Russe.

The same competition happened in London, but seasoned ballet-goers went, if in small numbers, to Les Ballets 1933. They knew in which direction the future lay. The company was forced to disband, and Balanchine, at 29, was once again without a company. He had, however, met Lincoln Kirstein.

Kirstein since the age of nine had been obsessed by the ballet and had even thought of running away and becoming a dancer, hardly an occupation for the son of a wealthy Boston family. Harvard was more suitable. In many ways he was in the Diaghilev mold. He was talented at painting and drawing, wrote poetry, published a novel and played the piano. But ballet, perhaps the best way to combine all these talents, interested him most.

A persuasive writer and polemicist of the ballet, he decided to bring ballet to

Above: The incident in Serenade *which Balanchine included after seeing a ballerina fall during rehearsal.*

Above right: Melissa Hayden, Maria Tallchief and Nicholas Magallanes in Serenade.

America. He did not know precisely how, but he obtained financial guarantees from wealthy backers and set sail for Europe. He had seen *La Chatte* and *Apollo* and knew that Balanchine was the man he wanted.

Romola Nijinsky, whom Kirstein had helped with her biography of her husband, arranged a meeting with Balanchine at the Savoy Theatre in 1933 and two days later firm proposals were made for Balanchine to go to America.

Balanchine arrived in America on 18 October 1933 and it is from this date that modern American ballet starts. This is not to do a disservice to other pioneers, but Balanchine did more than great choreography or great teaching. He set a style which was to become American through and through. On 1 January 1934 the School of American Ballet opened its doors in Isadora Duncan's old studios, with Balanchine as chairman of a teaching faculty of two: Dorothy Littlefield was American, Pierre Vladimirov had been Nijinsky's successor as leading male dancer at the Maryinsky.

The American Ballet, made up of the students from the school, gave its first performance in December 1934 in Hartford, Connecticut, the original planned home of the school. The program included ballets from Les Ballets 1933 together with a new work specially created to suit the talents of the students. This was *Serenade*, the first American masterpiece.

The story of Balanchine creating *Serenade* had passed into ballet legend. Balanchine's own view, perhaps tongue-in-cheek, was that 'I was just trying to teach my students some little lessons and make a ballet which wouldn't show how badly they danced,' but in this ballet he established what was referred to by Edwin Denby, the great American critic, as the young American look.

Balanchine went on to create other great ballets and worked once more with Stravinsky in the spring of 1937. This was the first Stravinsky Festival and included *Apollo*, *Le Baiser de la Fée* and *Jeu de Cartes*. The second monumental Stravinsky Festival took place in 1972 when almost every choreographable piece by Stravinsky was used.

Balanchine and Kirstein collaborated on various other ventures, such as Ballet Caravan, until 1939 following the dissolution of the American Ballet, and Balanchine choreographed for the stage and films, including the Rodgers and Hart musical *On Your Toes*.

Ballet Caravan was an important school for the up and coming American dancers and choreographers. From the combined forces of Ballet Caravan and what remained of the American Ballet, a joint company was formed to tour South America under the auspices of the government. It was at this time that Balanchine started to create the great 'neo-classical' ballets, founded on the style of *Apollo*, such as *Ballet Imperial* and *Concerto Barocco*.

Above: Mr Balanchine working with Igor Stravinsky.

Left: Suzanne Farrell and Peter Martins in Balanchine's choreography to Stravinsky's Violin Concerto.

Above: Daniel Duell, one of the young stars of the New York City Ballet, in Balanchine's Four Temperaments *to Hindemith's score.*

The tour came to an abrupt end with America's entry into the war. Kirstein was called up, as were most of the male dancers. To preserve the repertoire Kirstein offered the Balanchine ballets to Lucia Chase of American Ballet Theater, but she did not take them up and Balanchine took them with him to the Ballet Russe de Monte Carlo.

When Kirstein left the army in 1946 he once more joined forces with Balanchine and formed the Ballet Society which could call upon pupils of the school which Balanchine has continued to direct. From the repertoire of this company, which was largely dedicated to encouraging young choreographers, we still have three great Balanchine works – *Four Temperaments*, *Symphony in C* and *Orpheus*.

Ballet Society was given a base as part of the New York City Center. In 1948 it provided the dances for the productions by the New York City Opera and also gave ballet performances twice a week. The success of these performances led the city authorities to invite Kirstein and Balanchine to establish the ballet company as an independent organization.

The first performances of the New York City Ballet took place in October 1948. It was the culmination of 14 years of work by Kirstein and Balanchine and established Balanchine as the leading figure in American ballet.

It would be unfair to other dedicated workers to imply that little else was happening in America during these early years of the 1930s, but undoubtedly Balanchine dominated the scene choreographically and Kirstein was a true visionary. All other activity was on a sporadic basis and the only real advances were made by the greatly improved dancers and the opening of schools by dancers who stayed in America following the various tours of the Ballets Russes companies.

If all of Kirstein's efforts appear linked with Balanchine, it is also only fair to give full credit to his other ballet child: Ballet Caravan. This company brought to the fore three young American choreographers – Eugene Loring, Lew Christensen and William Dollar. Their ballets were concerned with American themes as opposed to Balanchine's international and universal approach.

Loring, born in Wisconsin, created *Billy the Kid*, a character ballet in one act which has become an American classic. It was produced in 1938, with a scenario by Kirstein and music by Aaron Copland. For many this is the first great all-American ballet and can be considered the forerunner of *Rodeo* created by Agnes de Mille for the Ballet Russe de Monte Carlo in 1942, again with a Copland score, following Massine's departure. This too is a watershed for American ballet as it marks the acceptance of the Ballet Russe company into the American dance scene. From then on it was essentially an American company in spite of its name.

Left: Marie Jeanne and Eugene Loring in the Ballet Caravan production of Billy the Kid.

Above: Melissa Hayden and William Dollar in his Le Combat *created in 1949 for the Ballet de Paris and later taken into the repertoire of American Ballet Theater as* The Duel.

Christensen produced *Filling Station*, described as a ballet-document, with a scenario by Kirstein and music by Virgil Thomson. Dollar worked more on general themes and was also a featured dancer at Radio City Music Hall.

Eugene Loring went on to produce ballets for Ballet Theater, now known as American Ballet Theater, and all three were involved in the early years of the New York City Ballet.

American Ballet Theater was organized in 1939 by Richard Pleasant who had worked with Mordkin and Lucia Chase, Mordkin's Lise in *La Fille Mal Gardée*. Pleasant promoted his new company with typical American *brio*. It was billed as being '. . . staged by the greatest collaboration in ballet history' and brought together dancers from the Mordkin Ballet with its important repertoire and Russian connections, Fokine who staged *Carnaval* and *Les Sylphides* (from which production Dame Alicia Markova's present-day production derives) and Anton Dolin who mounted *Giselle* and *Swan Lake* Act 2. Pleasant also announced a total company of 91, a Spanish unit of 19, a Negro unit of 14, 11 designers, three conductors and the works of 18 composers!

Left: Agnes de Mille created a whole body of work concerned with the American experience, including Rodeo *and, left,* Harvest According *danced by Jenny Workman and Kelly Brown, father of Lesley Brown. It was an extension of her ballet in the musical* Bloomer Girl.

Important American works were created by de Mille and Loring while Anthony Tudor and Andrée Howard revived works from the Ballet Rambert and London Ballet repertoire. It was altogether a sensational first season. The company met with instant public approval and established itself as the truly American company, a position it has maintained over the years. Its policy of continuous touring has, until very recently, meant that to the great mass of Americans across the continent ballet was American Ballet Theater, whatever the international prestige of New York City Ballet.

Within three years a new choreographic pattern was already establishing itself, although the classics and a 'star' policy (which brought Markova, Dolin, Baronova, Riabouchinska and Eglevsky to the American public) were of paramount importance. Apart from her essentially American themes, de Mille broke new ground with *Obeah*, using Milhaud's *La Création du Monde*, for the Negro unit. Tudor rediscovered himself and set to work on *Dim Lustre* and *Pillar of Fire* as well as the important revivals of *Dark Elegies*, *Lilac Garden* and *Judgment of Paris*. From the ranks of the company Jerome Robbins emerged.

Tudor's influence on ballet developed in America, particularly in his exploration of

Above: Natalia Makarova and Gayle Young in Tudor's Lilac Garden, *which he mounted for American Ballet Theater in 1940.*

Above right: Nora Kaye and Hugh Laing in Pillar of Fire *(1942), Tudor's first major work after his arrival in America and regarded by many as his masterpiece.*

psychological themes and how to express them. *Pillar of Fire* with music by Schoenberg, has a definite story: a woman who loves, but loses her love to her prettier, younger sister. In desperation at the thought of being a loveless spinster she has a brief liaison with an inexperienced young man, which makes her feel unworthy of her first love when he returns to her with love and sincerity. The ballet is full of realistic, almost casual gestures, but is firmly based on the classical technique. Nora Kaye gave a powerful performance as the heroine, a performance which marked her out as one of the new generation of dramatic American dancers.

Dim Lustre has only a slight plot and the characters are described and not named: the Lady with Him and the Gentleman with Her. Small incidents during their dance in a ballroom – a kiss, a dropped handkerchief – evoke fleeting memories of past events and past partners. The moments of change from past to present are shown by a dimming of the lights, a time-stop mechanism reminiscent of his brilliant invention in *Lilac Garden*, a moment of absolute stillness freezing the heroine's drama.

Tudor went on to create *Undertow, Romeo and Juliet* and then, in 1948, *Shadow of the Wind*. The circumstances surrounding the creation of this ballet were strange and marked a new way of working for Tudor. He had always planned meticulously, but this time he left almost everything until the last moment. Agnes de Mille writes that two days before the premiere there was over 45 minutes of music to arrange. It is possible that this marked the sad decline in his powers which dogged him for 15 years. He left American Ballet Theater in 1950 and took over the direction of the Metropolitan Opera Ballet. At the same time Hugh Laing, Diana Adams and Nora Kaye also left to join New York City Ballet. There Jerome Robbins was already an associate artistic director. Robbins had started dancing at the age of 19 studying mainly free dance with a little ballet on the side. He also studied Spanish and Oriental dancing, gaining a thorough background for a career which would use all of these to the full. He began to choreograph early and during summer schools created ballets based on French farce and high drama. He supported himself before he joined American Ballet Theater by dancing in Broadway shows. One had choreography by Balanchine – *Keep Off the Grass*. In ABT dramatic talents as a dancer were recognized and he danced such important roles as Petrouchka, Mercutio in *Romeo and Juliet* and in *Billy the Kid*. His greatest early role he created for himself, as one of the three sailors in *Fancy Free*.

The concept of *Fancy Free* owed much to the pioneer work of Agnes de Mille in this field, as well as *Billy the Kid*. De Mille had by now produced and expanded *Rodeo* and had also created one of the most important dance sequences in the history of that all-American art, the musical. The dream sequence in *Oklahoma* was the first of its type. Unlike previous ballets it expanded the character and the story.

For *Fancy Free* Robbins prepared the scenario in great detail and wrote out the plot on almost filmic lines, much the same as de Mille had done. His particular gift for developing this technique was to introduce natural gestures in a particular relaxed and casual manner. He was also able to create a flow of movement which went through the dance passages, some of great virtuosity, into the non-dance sections. At this early age Robbins was the master of artlessness. Every move looked completely natural no matter what care and calculation had gone into it. In the same year *Fancy Free* was expanded into a full-length stage musical, *On the Town*. Robbins collaborated with Betty Comden and Adolph Green, and was to spend as much of his time in the future in the world of the musical as in the ballet, with great benefit to both.

His next ballet venture was *Interplay*, made originally for Billy Rose's Concert Varieties and then taken into the ABT repertoire; his next musical was the lively *High Button Shoes* in 1947. Before this he attempted a serious psychological study, *Facsimile*, which, through the changing relationships between its three characters, sought to show the emptiness of modern life. The choreography lacked the free-flowing inventiveness of his early works and appeared too obvious in its gestures.

He joined the NYCB in 1949 as associate director and immediately made another attempt at a serious work, *The Guests*, which explored the tension between rival groups, at the time assumed to refer to anti-semitism. It was a theme he referred to in another medium, his great musical *West Side Story* (1957) which changed the whole face of musical theater. Obviously the theme of conflict, or perhaps the eternal wish of the clown to play tragedy, still intrigued him and his next major ballet was *The Age of Anxiety* set to Leonard Bernstein's second symphony and W.H. Auden's dramatic poem of the same title. With the exception of the Masque scene this ballet, too, proved less than clear. The message was simple. Robbins was best at creating *dancing*.

From the period up to 1959 the works which have lasted include the beautiful *Afternoon of a Faun*, in which a narcissistic male dancer sees his nymph in the shape of a ballerina; *The Cage*, made for the powerful Nora Kaye, an overblown allegorical piece about the female being deadlier than the male; and *The Concert* – simply an

Below: Michael Coleman in the Royal Ballet production of Robbins' The Concert.

Above: The original cast of Robbins' Fancy Free *(John Kriza, Harold Lang and Robbins) bow to the cast which danced at the gala to celebrate 35 years of American Ballet Theater (Fernando Bujones, Terry Orr and Buddy Balogh).*

extremely funny ballet. The daydreams of the audience at a recital of Chopin achieve a controlled madness full of brilliant invention.

Before creating *West Side Story* Robbins had choreographed the ballet *The Small House of Uncle Tom* for both the stage and film versions of *The King and I*, as well as the musical *Peter Pan*. Soon after he created his own company, Ballets USA, which made its debut at the Spoleto Festival in Italy in 1958. For this company he created *Moves*, danced in silence, and *NY Export: Opus Jazz*. Robbins made further productions for the stage, such as *Fiddler on the Roof*, before making a controversial come-back to ballet with *Les Noces* for ABT. After a two-year period of experimentation he returned to NYCB as a choreographer.

His next major choreography, in 1969, was *Dances at a Gathering*, to a selection of Chopin piano pieces. This inventive and moving kaleidoscope of dance showed Robbins returning to the classical vein once more. Since then he has produced many ballets for the company, including *Goldberg Variations*, *Mother Goose* and *Piano Concerto in G* (the latter pair being his contribution to the Ravel Festival of 1975).

Robbins is still one of the three ballet masters of NYCB and has worked alongside George Balanchine for the best part of 30 years. His innate craftsmanship and theatricality have happily developed alongside the genius of Balanchine, complementing his more cerebral style perfectly.

Once NYCB was established in 1948 Balanchine set about reviving his own works and polishing them to perfection. Unnecessary costuming was discarded and stylized practice tights became the NYCB uniform. It was not long before emotive titles vanished too. *Ballet Imperial* became *Piano Concerto No 3*; all traces of its former connection with the grandeur of the Imperial court were wiped out, except those contained within the choreography. Balanchine believed in essentials and the only time his unerring instinct has failed him was when he planned a production of *Les Sylphides* in practice dress. It did not work.

Plot ballets are rare in the Balanchine repertoire. *Prodigal Son* and *Orpheus* were early exceptions and he has produced a full-length *Don Quixote* (with an original score by Nikolas Nabokov). Uninterested in dramatic dancing, his concern has been entirely musical. He is always quoted as saying that choreography is easy. All you have to do is listen to the music. For him this is certainly true and it has not restricted his range of styles. For some his style can be too crisp, too precise and impersonal, but the innate musicality and inventiveness bring the ballets to a peak of perfection. He prefers, in his own words, music which is pure and heartless, to be admired rather than to excite emotions. His dancers are trained to dance steps, not emote. Everything necessary will be put into the steps by Balanchine and no embellishment or 'selling' by the dancer will be needed.

Having maintained control over the School of American Ballet, Balanchine has been able to train generations of dancers to his ideal standard. The first ballerinas of the company were not uniform, but in them can be seen the qualities he was to heighten and develop in his future pupils. Melissa Hayden, Jillana and Maria Tallchief were not obviously in his mold, while Diana Adams, Allegra Kent and Tanquil LeClerq were. They were the forerunners of the slim, long-legged virtuosos we know today: Suzanne Farrell, Kay Mazzo and Gelsey Kirkland. Of his present-day ballerinas only Patricia McBride has something of an 'international' look.

Mr Balanchine's pursuit of the art of the ballerina has led him to neglect the male dancer and it is only in recent years that he has made up for this deficiency. His interest has always been in the ballerina as woman idealized. He was not able to find such inspiration from men, which, given the available talent across America from his earliest days, is surprising. He took to everything American instantly, switching from the natty gents' suiting he affected in London to cowboy jackets with perfect ease when he first arrived, but he did not see the dance possibilities of the American male. The virile style of Robbins as in *Fancy Free* suited the outgoing American dancers perfectly. They looked right as sailors. Perhaps Balanchine knew instinctively that it would be a while before they looked at home in his cool neo-classical ballets.

American Ballet Theater encouraged young male dancers such as John Kriza and Michael Kidd (who produced some brilliant choreography for films such as *Seven Brides for Seven Brothers*) while a new generation of dancers grew in NYCB. They were all of particularly manly appearance and helped increase the number of boys who were allowed by conservative parents to take up dance. Jacques d'Amboise, the first great American male dancer with NYCB, was soon joined by Arthur Mitchell, who went on to create the Dance Theater of Harlem, and Edward Villella, perhaps the greatest publicist for the cause of male dancing in America. Short, athletic and with an exciting technique he made Balanchine's *Prodigal Son* his own, and excelled in modern works such as *Agon* and the later, deeply contemplative, *Watermill* by Robbins.

When NYCB attracted Robbins and Tudor left, together with some leading dancers, ABT was without a 'house' choreographer. Even John Taras, one of the triumvirate running NYCB, left having received his earliest opportunities there. His main contribution to ballet, with the exception of one florid piece of choreography, *Piège de Lumière* for Rosella Hightower and the *Ballet du Marquis de Cuevas*, was ultimately as a producer of Balanchine's works throughout the world.

ABT lost direction during the 1950s, but maintained a good international repertoire and continued to produce its own dancers including one great ballerina, the Cuban, Alicia Alonso. Cut off from her American base by political difficulties she eventually devoted all her time to the Cuban National Ballet, a technically formidable, Russian trained group, she had founded in 1948.

ABT enjoyed periods of great activity, interspersed with the problems of fund-raising. No great choreographers emerged from its ranks and it was forced to import most of its talent.

Ballet and Modern Dance Today

Russia

Ballet in Russia is a massive state enterprise centering on the great companies at the Bolshoi Theater in Moscow and the Kirov Theater in Leningrad. From these spread out a network of small and large companies across the country from Tiflis to Perm, Kiev to Novosibirsk. Each company has an associated school, the best graduates inevitably gravitating toward the two main companies. Similarly, dancers of soloist grade are sent from Moscow or Leningrad to strengthen the ranks of the smaller companies.

The company in Perm, directed by Boyarchikov, is one of the few of these to have made appearances outside Russia and also, a rarer event, has had one of its productions, *Romeo and Juliet*, taken into the repertoire of a Western company (West Berlin). Among the products of its school is Nadezhda Pavlova, the fragile-looking ballerina with a brilliant technique who first came to international notice when she won the International Ballet Competition in Moscow in 1974. A fellow winner, Boris Godunov, is a typical product of the company in Riga, as was Vladimir Gelvan. Godunov now dances with the Bolshoi Ballet, as does Pavlova. Gelvan left Russia and had success with American Ballet Theater in ballets such as *Raymonda*, before joining the company in West Berlin, which is headed by Valery and Galina Panov.

The company in Riga, the national company of fiercely independent Latvia, has

Bottom left: Nadezhda Pavlova and Marat Daukayev in the Perm Ballet production of Romeo and Juliet.

Bottom center: Maya Plisetskaya and Nikolai Fadeyechev in Lavrovsky's production of Grigorovich's The Stone Flower.

Bottom right: The Maly Ballet production of Stravinsky's The Rite of Spring *with Abdyev as The Shepherd. Since Stravinsky's music became acceptable in the Soviet Union, there have also been productions of* The Firebird *and* Petrouchka.

also produced other great male dancers like Maris Liepa and Mikhail Baryshnikov. Perhaps the greatest male dancer of his generation as well as choreographer of roles for men was Vakhtang Chaboukiani who worked in Tiflis, his birthplace. One of his best known ballets is *Laurencia* which he also produced in Kiev. It is rarely danced outside Russia, but the divertissement from the wedding scene has been produced by both Rudolf Nureyev and Galina Samsova. She was trained in Kiev and was a soloist there before leaving Russia to dance first in Canada, then Paris, before making her home in Britain.

There is also a large company in Novosibirsk, in the fastest growing Soviet state, Siberia. Under the direction of Vinagradov, productions of *Cinderella* and *Romeo and Juliet* made a great impression in 1964 and 1965 and the company has already made a foreign tour. Vinogradov went on to direct the Maly (small) Ballet in Leningrad which is really the Leningrad City Ballet, the Kirov being a state company. This company has attempted productions which were thought a little avant-garde within Russia, as well as revivals of Petipa and other classical works, and made a very strong impression when it first appeared in Paris. Igor Belsky, one of the group of choreographers connected with this company, who was artistic director for nearly 10 years before Vinogradov, made important new productions of the Russian classic *The Little Hump-backed Horse* as well as Shostakovich's *Ninth Symphony* in 1966. He went on to direct the Kirov Ballet which still reigns supreme as the home of glorious classical dancing.

Left: Two scenes from the massive Bolshoi Ballet production of Spartacus *by Grigorovich. Top: Mikhail Lavrovsky as Spartacus. Bottom: Ekaterina Maximova mourns over the dead Spartacus.*

Right: Maya Plisetskaya rehearsing with Maris Liepa for her own ballet, Anna Karenina.

The strength of the company is based on the firm foundations of the school, the Vaganova Institute, which carries on the work of that great teacher. An account of its work and a clear indication of the superb talent it gathers together, both the precocious children and the dedicated teachers, is shown in the film *The Children of Theatre Street*. Sadly the outlets for the brilliant dancers which are produced are limited artistically since the policies of the Kirov company have been sterile for some time, though there have been recent attempts to infuse new life. Roland Petit has mounted a version of *The Hunchback of Notre Dame* for them, but the company's own choreographers have great difficulty in achieving a balance between what is politically acceptable and what they would really like to do.

The lack of real creativity played a great part in the decision by some of the company's brightest young stars, including Nureyev, Makarova and Baryshnikov, to leave Russia. Products of the Vaganova School, their noble classical style and unforced open technique find an immediate sympathy in the West, which is natural as much of Western classical dance has drawn its inspiration from the Leningrad School through the first generation of dancers to leave Russia with Diaghilev. These Kirov dancers who have chosen to work outside Russia have found that their style blends easily with that of their new companies. Only Galina and Valery Panov have had difficulty adapting, probably because Panov was a brilliant character dancer within Russia and he was expected to shine as a pure classicist when he arrived in the West.

The resilience of the Kirov company is remarkable considering that there has been a constant history of important talents leaving for Moscow since Ulanova moved there in 1944. The dancers now include Irina Kolpakova, Vaganova's last pupil, Alla Sizova and Vladimir Semenyov, but as yet there is not the wealth of new talent on the horizon as in the recent past. The loss of three great dancers left an enormous gap, as did the death of Yuri Soloviev in 1977. He had made a most notable debut, dancing the *Bluebird pas de deux* with Makarova, and his soaring jump and elegant style made him one of the most popular dancers with the company.

The choreographer, Grigorovich, also made his important first ballets with the Kirov company before leaving for Moscow in 1964, including *The Stone Flower* and *The Legend of Love*. The Bolshoi Ballet has made a more conscious effort to produce new works over recent years with varying degrees of success. The most popular has been Grigorovich's production of *Spartacus* in 1968, the theme of which (the slaves' uprising against the might of imperial Rome) had an obvious appeal in Russia, although it does have various interpretations. There had been attempts to choreograph Aram Khatachurian's lush score before, but only young Grigorovich succeeded in devising a construction which worked – intimate scenes for the principal protagonists alternating with powerful mass movements for the slaves and Roman legions. It provided unique roles for Ekaterina Maximova, Vladimir Vassiliev, Maris Liepa and Nina Timofeyeva, the reigning Bolshoi stars, alongside Natalia Bessmertnova, Mikhail Lavrovsky, the young Vyatchyslav Gordeyev, Boris Akimov and Maya Plisetskaya.

Above: Vladimir Vassiliev in Ivan the Terrible *by Grigorovich.*

Right: Yuri Vladimirov as Ivan and Natalia Bessmertnova as Anastasia in Ivan the Terrible.

Plisetskaya assumed the title of prima ballerina following Ulanova's retirement and has been particularly successful in walking the tightrope between conformity and innovation. Not all of her new ideas were successful, but she must be applauded for taking an independent line. She has danced outside Russia in ballets which she could not expect to perform at home, such as Roland Petit's creation *La Rose Malade*, and Béjart's *Bolero*, and has imported choreography not firmly in the Russian mold. Alberto Alonso, the Cuban choreographer, made *Carmen* for her using a rearrangement of Bizet's tunes by her husband Rodion Schedrin. He also wrote the score for her own attempt at choreography in *Anna Karenina* in 1972. In 1975 Grigorovich attempted to repeat the successful formula of *Spartacus*, but although there were scenes of great splendor and a commanding central role, *Ivan the Terrible* did not make the same impact, in spite of Prokofiev's music, drawn largely from his score for the famous film by Eisenstein.

Above: Vassiliev rehearsing his own ballet, Icarus.

Right: Maximova and Vassiliev in the last pas de deux *from* Icarus.

Below: Loipa Araujo, winner of the Gold Medal at the Varna Competition in 1965, and now ballerina with the Cuban Ballet.

Apart from the natural influence of style through teaching, perhaps best shown in Japan, the Russian ballet has had a direct influence along political lines across Eastern Europe and in Cuba. Companies such as those in Sofia and Bucharest rely heavily on Russian, and particularly the athletic Bolshoi, style and choreography. Other companies, such as those in Prague and Budapest, have enjoyed greater freedom. Choreographers such as Pavel Smok were given opportunities in Czechoslovakia and Merce Cunningham made appearances there in 1964; visiting modern dance companies such as Ballet Rambert always arouse particular interest. The company in Budapest relied heavily on Soviet productions such as Vainonen's *Flames of Paris* and *The Nutcracker* for many years, but recently they have encouraged choreographers from the West and their repertoire now includes works by Ashton (*La Fille Mal Gardée*), Lander (*Etudes*) and Béjart (*Firebird*), often danced by visiting ballerinas such as Maina Gielgud. Their own dancers, too, have frequently appeared with Western companies. Viktor Rona has partnered Margot Fonteyn and worked closely with the Norwegian Ballet and Imre Dózsa has made particularly charming appearances with London Festival Ballet and the Royal Swedish Ballet.

Bulgaria hosts the International Competition at Varna, the first of these events, which now include even more elaborate ones in Moscow and Tokyo. Many young dancers have been brought to international notice there and it has proved a useful show-case for new talent from Japan and Cuba. The Japanese dancers, though they have certain limitations in classical line, are invariably technically outstanding. Few have made extensive careers in Europe and America, but at home there are countless companies, the most notable of which are the Tokyo Ballet and the Asami Maki Ballet, organized by Madam Maki, one of Japan's great ballerinas.

Cuba has a strong company headed by the ballerina Alicia Alonso and her husband Fernando, with brother-in-law Alberto as choreographer. The associated school has produced most of the present generation of dancers who have replaced the largely American personnel of the 1950s and early 1960s. The ballerina Loipa Araujo has performed as a guest in Europe with Roland Petit in Marseilles and the company makes frequent tours. Alicia Alonso still performs and for many is the greatest Giselle. A relaxation in the political situation has meant that once more she and her company have been able to perform in New York, enjoying an outstanding success in 1978.

Rudolf Nureyev

The widely publicized, not to say over-publicized, 'leap to freedom' which Rudolf Nureyev took at Paris Airport in 1961 resulted in unprecedented exposure for the art of dance. Not since the days of Nijinsky had a dancer made news on such a scale. In real life the incident was somewhat less dramatic and had even been expected by close friends of the dancer.

His defection provided ballet in the West with a very strong boost. From a complacent point of view things might have looked very healthy – the standard of dancing at the Royal Ballet was high. Nureyev's arrival, however, had an inestimable effect on male dancing, inspired by both rivalry and comparison. Margot Fonteyn was the undisputed prima ballerina, but one only has to read her own biography to see that she considered herself on the way down. Nureyev gave her career and art a new lease of life. An added bonus was his effect on audiences who might never otherwise have ventured to the ballet. If they only went to gawk at the defector with the unpronounceable name, they left knowing they had seen a truly great dancer.

Rudolf Nureyev was a relatively late starter; in fact, considering the difficulties, it seems amazing he started at all. That he did must have been from an early desire to dance, but since most of his youth (he was born in 1938) coincided with the years of

Left: The young Nureyev rehearsing with Sergeyev, whose roles he inherited, and his teacher Pushkin.

deprivation as a result of Russia's entry into the Second World War, there was little opportunity to find an outlet for it. In any case when his father returned from the war he was not keen that his son should become a dancer.

But by this time Nureyev had had dancing lessons, mostly in Russian folk dance, in his home town of Ufa and he had been inspired by the ballerina Nazvedtinova at his local Opera House. He had even managed to get on stage as an extra and also had the audacity to earn money giving dance classes at the local workers' collective.

He was eventually taken on as an apprentice dancer, thanks to the enthusiasm of his teachers, and toured with the company, soon making his first trip to Moscow. This was not the aim of his teachers, who strongly recommended him to the Vaganova Academy attached to the Kirov Theater in Leningrad. This aim seemed to him altogether too much to hope for. He had, however, some idea of the Leningrad style as soloists from there had been evacuated to Ufa, which by all accounts had a good reputation as a ballet company.

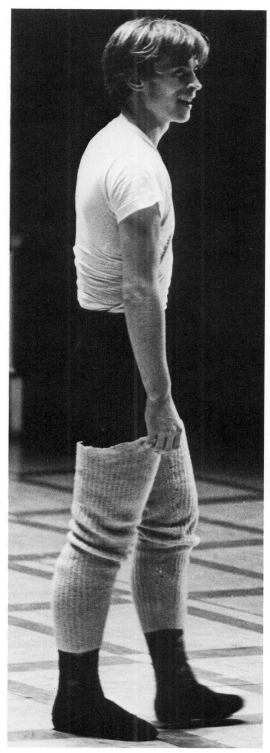

Nureyev rehearsing for one of Margot Fonteyn's galas in aid of the Royal Academy of Dancing.

He continued to work like a madman, learning everything he possibly could, something he continued to do long after his establishment as a dancer of international stature. This hard work was rewarded when he was ensured a place as part of the Ufa company taking part in a festival in Moscow. When the arrangements were being made the young Nureyev, with only five minutes' rehearsal, replaced an injured soloist in a difficult solo in the ballet *The Song of the Crane*.

Once in Moscow he went to take classes with Asaf Messerer, but was formally examined for a place in the school by another teacher. He was offered a place in the eighth grade, one below the highest. For purely practical reasons (he would have had to find his own accommodation in Moscow) and perhaps a feeling that the Leningrad style would suit him better, he bought a one-way ticket to Leningrad, only to find the company away on vacation. However, he was able to pass the time visiting museums and galleries with a relative of his teacher from Ufa.

His entrance examination took place in August 1955 and he was accepted as a student, but only in the sixth grade. This upset him, not only as he had been offered eighth grade in Moscow, but as it would mean that he might not graduate into the company before being called up for military service, which would ruin his career. He objected and made his point, but was marked out as a difficult pupil who tended to go his own way. He did however find a sympathetic teacher in Alexander Pushkin.

In his final year an opportunity came to show his progress when the main company was away and he was able to dance principal roles with Alla Sizova in the theater, roles such as the Nutcracker Prince. In June 1958 he danced three very different solos in a competition in Moscow – having to repeat one, such was his success – surrounded by such young talent as Makorova dancing with Soloviev and Maximova with Vassiliev. At the suggestion of David Blair, Frederick Ashton used some steps from the film of this competition in *La Fille Mal Gardée*, a ballet Nureyev danced in later years.

As a result of his success Nureyev was offered contracts in Moscow, but was also offered not only a contract but the chance to dance with Natalia Dudinskaya, the prima ballerina at the Kirov. He accepted, sure that he would have greater artistic freedom there. He made his debut in *Laurencia*, from which only the wedding divertissement dances are seen in the West. He also soon made one of his first appearances outside Russia: at a Youth Festival in Vienna.

His interests outside the Kirov, whether in visiting companies or simply in having a separate life, continued to draw criticism and as a result he was sent to tour East Germany (with a circus!) when the company went on a major Russian Tour. As a result he missed the American Ballet Theater when they visited Russia, but he did manage to see a film of Erik Bruhn who became a major influence after his defection. He regarded Bruhn, the great Danish classicist, as the world's leading male dancer, a view he did not change in spite of his own popularity in later years.

Before the company left for their visit to Paris in 1961 he had danced many more major roles in ballets such as *Don Quixote* and *Gayaneh*, as well as the classics *Swan*

Lake and *The Sleeping Beauty*. He also danced and, perhaps most importantly, made seriously thought-out changes to *Giselle* and *La Bayadere*, changes which have been approved both in Russia and the West and are now accepted parts of the ballets.

He was surprised to be included in the company for the Paris tour but it appears that the formidable Minister of Culture at the time, Mme Furtseva, favored showing Russia's brightest ballet talent rather than Dudinskaya and Sergeyev, much to the annoyance of audiences in Paris and London. The repertoire was big enough to show off old favorites as well as new talent.

Nureyev's impact on Paris was electrifying for both public and critics alike. He knew that he was being watched when he went his own way to the Opéra and museums or when simply making new friends. He was suspicious at the airport when he was shown his ticket, an unusual procedure, as though to reassure him. At the last moment Sergeyev told him that he was needed in Moscow for a special performance and would join the company in London later. Nureyev knew that this would mean the end of overseas visits for him. A friend seeing him off guessed what he was thinking and she informed the French police, who escorted him to a room where he could make up his mind freely.

The rest of the story has become an integral part of the growth of both ballet and modern dance throughout the world.

Above: Nureyev has been adventurous in his choice of modern roles, which have ranged from Tetley's Pierrot Lunaire, *above, to* Lucifer, *specially created for him by Martha Graham.*

Britain, Canada, Australia

With the Royal Ballet established at the Royal Opera House at Covent Garden – the 'Royal' accolade granted by charter in 1956 – British ballet was as much established as a state institution as any Soviet company. It was, however, able to work with complete freedom, other than a dependence on the government for financial assistance. Extensive American tours, which followed the spectacular success of the 1949 season, brought in valuable income, much of which unfortunately became merged with the income of the Opera House as a whole, a source of constant complaint in the ballet press. Frederick Ashton continued to be the chief choreographer and eventually became director on the retirement of the founding director Ninette de Valois in 1963. The responsibilities of organizing a huge company limited his choreographic output, but during this period he produced the two *pas de trois* which make up *Monotones* and the peculiarly English *Enigma Variations* which brought to life the friends of the composer Edward Elgar pictured in his music.

Below: Frederick Ashton's The Dream *choreographed in 1964. It is danced here by Merle Park and Anthony Dowell, who created the role of Oberon.*

Ashton was succeeded as director of the Royal Ballet in 1970 by Kenneth Macmillan and John Field, who soon left to direct the ballet at La Scala, Milan. He had been responsible for the smaller, touring company of the Royal Ballet, having been a dancer with the company himself, which travelled the length and breadth of Britain for over 40 weeks each year. This invaluable little company produced its own dancers – there was little interchange with Covent Garden – such as Christopher Gable and David Wall as well as its own ballerina, Doreen Wells.

Kenneth Macmillan was one of the postwar generation of British choreographers which included John Cranko and Peter Darrell. He was born in Dunfermline, Scotland, and trained at the Sadler's Wells Ballet School, joining the company as a dancer, but working soon after with the Sadler's Wells Theater Ballet, based at that theater. His first work, apart from workshop productions, for the company was *Danses Concertantes* in 1955. This witty and sparkling work made an instant impact and was followed soon after by the highly dramatic *House of Birds*. His career since then has managed to mix these two themes and has culminated in his interest in the form of the full-length ballet.

Left: Kenneth Macmillan's Song of the Earth *in the Royal Ballet production with Anthony Dowell, and Donald Macleary and Marcia Haydée in the role she created in Stuttgart.*

In 1958 he created *The Burrow* for the young Canadian dancer, Lynn Seymour, which was to be the start of a mutually creative partnership. Most of his ballets after this were created for her, including *The Invitation*, in which her portrayal of the destruction of innocence was extremely moving, and *Romeo and Juliet*. The premiere was danced by Margot Fonteyn and Rudolf Nureyev in 1965, but the dramatic concept of Juliet had been created on Seymour and her style showed through the choreography. In 1966 Macmillan went to direct the ballet at the West Berlin Opera House, taking Lynn Seymour and other dancers with him. It was here that he produced the one-act version of *Anastasia* in which Seymour portrayed Anna Andersen, the woman who claims to be Anastasia. Soon after his return to London to direct the Royal Ballet Macmillan expanded this into the first of a series of full-length works that included *Manon* in 1974 and most recently *Mayerling*. He was succeeded by Norman Morrice as director of the Royal Ballet in 1978, but continues to choreograph. His works are found in the repertoires of many major companies and one of his greatest, *Das Lied von der Erde*, was created for a foreign company at the invitation of John Cranko in Stuttgart, before being taken into the repertoire of the Royal Ballet. He returned to Stuttgart to create *Requiem* in memory of Cranko. Both these works have a quality of stillness and sadness quite unlike the bulk of the works made for his own company.

Above: Lynn Seymour as Anna Andersen in the original one-act version of Anastasia.

Right: Kenneth Macmillan's latest controversial full-length ballet Mayerling, *with David Wall and Lynn Seymour as the Crown Prince Rudolph and his mistress.*

Outside the Royal Ballet, activity in the postwar years centered around the Ballet Rambert, the International Ballet of Mona Inglesby and the Metropolitan Ballet which introduced Erik Bruhn, Sonia Arova and the young Svetlana Beriosova to British audiences. By the beginning of the 1950s only Ballet Rambert remained a serious influence. In 1946 they had staged a particularly successful version of *Giselle* and in 1947–48 made an artistically successful tour of Australia and New Zealand which almost ruined them financially. Their principal dancers, Belinda Wright and John Gilpin, later became part of the Festival Ballet of Markova and Dolin, but Marie Rambert succeeded, as ever, in finding outstanding new talent in Paula Hinton and then Lucette Aldous. She also found a new choreographer in Norman Morrice and he proved vital in the transition of the company from classical to modern when touring large productions became well-nigh impossible. Though these were invariably of a very high standard, *La Sylphide* by Elsa Marianne von Rosen and *Don Quixote* being good examples, the financial problems were too great for such a small company. The last performance of the 'classical' Ballet Rambert took place on 2 July 1966. Just over two weeks later the 'modern' Ballet Rambert emerged with Norman Morrice as its artistic head.

Above: Glen Tetley's Field Figures *for the Royal Ballet, one of his first creations for a purely classical company.*

Marie Rambert still inspires the company and takes a considerable interest in new productions. These have been very many and, like the Nederlands Dans Theater with which it has much in common, the emphasis is on a constantly vital and changing repertoire. Ballet Rambert was instrumental in bringing Glen Tetley to work in Britain and he has produced some of his most creative works for them, consolidating his position as one of the leading modern choreographers in Europe. Curiously enough he does not have this position in America and has only made inroads into the dance scene there through classical companies and classical dancers. As with Nederlands Dans Theater he has found that classically trained dancers, with the added burnish of modern technique, are the perfect exponents of what he has to say and he has built on this, rather like Hans van Manen has, from works such as *Mythical Hunters* through to *Voluntaries* for the Royal Ballet, *Gemini* for the Australian Ballet and now the full-length *The Tempest* for Ballet Rambert once more.

Ballet Rambert have also produced their own choreographer in Christopher Bruce, who is also one of the great modern dancers. He belongs to no particular school of modern dance, which has left him free to create particularly fluid dances as well as important pieces of dance drama such as *Cruel Garden*, based on the life story of the Spanish poet Garcia Lorca. He is now the director of the company, as well as principal dancer and choreographer. His ballets have not found a wide outlet away from his own company, but they can be seen in Cologne and Munich.

Below: Lucy Burge in Smiling Immortal *by Norman Morrice.*

Left: Michael Ho as The Moon in Christopher Bruce's large-scale production of Cruel Garden, *created in collaboration with the mime, Lindsay Kemp.*

In the period before the Festival of Britain in 1951 Alicia Markova and Anton Dolin together with the impresario Julian Braunsweg formed the Festival Ballet, now London Festival Ballet. This company has had a checkered financial and artistic history but under the direction of Beryl Grey achieved a great measure of stability and success. For the first time in its history it has a permanent base with excellent studios and it is building up a strong company from *corps de ballet* to principals. From the earliest days it has been headed largely by guest dancers, but has always had room for home-developed talent. When Markova left in 1952 Belinda Wright took over as ballerina and John Gilpin, the most stylish dancer of his generation, led the male dancers for many years. Danilova, Toumanova, Riabouchinska and Toni Lander have danced with the company, which for much of the 1960s and 1970s was headed by the Russian ballerina Galina Samsova who was usually partnered by Andre Prokovsky. It has yet to produce a ballerina from its own ranks directly (the charming Gaye Fulton is the nearest yet, but she had a period abroad before returning as a ballerina), but it should not be long before it does so.

Northern Dance Theatre has been surprisingly successful in creating a small-scale touring repertoire with versions of the classics very cleverly scaled down as well as tailored to suit their local audience. Scottish Ballet has developed into a major 'national' company with a wide repertoire of classics, often in Darrell's idiosyncratic versions, as well as Bournonville ballets such as *La Sylphide*, a natural choice for Scotland, and *Napoli* as well as the less known *La Ventana*. The national character of the company was emphasized in an interesting production of *Mary Queen of Scots* with music by Thea Musgrave which Darrell added to his list of original full-length works that include *Beauty and the Beast* and *The Tales of Hoffmann*. The company has an important educational group and both branches show works in the modern idiom alongside the classics.

Left: Elaine MacDonald in Bournonville's Napoli *mounted for the Scottish Ballet by Poul Gnatt. The repertoire also includes Hans Brenaa's well-known production of* La Sylphide.

Above: A scene from People *by Robert Cohan, former partner of Martha Graham and director of the London Contemporary Dance Theatre.*

Overleaf: Christopher Bruce as Prospero in Glen Tetley's full-length The Tempest *to a score by Arne Nordheim for Ballet Rambert.*

Overleaf right: London Contemporary Dance Theatre in Robert Cohan's Cell.

Modern dance in Britain was very slow to take root and owes much to one man, Robin Howard, and the inspiration of Martha Graham. Her visit to London in 1954 was not a great public success in terms of attendances, but the few who did attend became fervent disciples. A later tour of Europe by Graham did not include London but Howard, who had been overwhelmed by her in 1954, determined to make it possible and with his own money and the backing he acquired, the season took place. It was a stunning success and almost overnight, as the result of a few performances and a lecture demonstration by Graham, Britain really discovered modern dance.

Howard determined to build on this success and, following visits by other modern dance companies such as Paul Taylor and Alvin Ailey, he was instrumental in setting up a trust fund (largely again with his own money) to organize scholarships for British dancers to study with Graham in New York and eventually to open a full-time school with Robert Cohan, Martha Graham's partner, as director. This school, The Place, became the center of modern dance activity in Britain and from it grew the performing arm of the enterprise – the London Contemporary Dance Theatre.

Inevitably in the early years much of the creative activity was American inspired and the company drew from the American experience dancers such as Naomi Lapzeson and William Louther as well as Cohan itself. Louther soon turned to choreography as well as dancing and from its own ranks the company produced Barry Moreland, who moved on to work in the classical field, and Robert North, who came from the classical ballet, and Richard Alston, who broke away to form his own group Strider. As with the modern dance scene throughout the world these small groups come and go, but it is often from them that new ideas develop.

If Britain had to import a ready-made modern tradition, it has made a major export business out of the classical ballet and companies throughout the world including Canada and Australia come within its sphere of influence.

Europe

While modern dance maintained a toehold in most European countries immediately before the war, the fortunes of the classical ballet had to wait until peacetime to take hold in countries such as Sweden, Germany, Holland and Belgium. By this time a revival was already taking place in France and ballet was enjoying a particularly inventive period. In Britain ballet was soon to be firmly established in the Opera House and to be granted a Royal Charter. Its schools played an important part in supplying dancers to the growing companies of Germany and it also provided its single most influential figure, John Cranko.

Ballet in Germany suffered largely from the Opera House system, and had an unhappy relationship with the dominant opera. Companies were not given time to grow because of the endless game of musical chairs played by the Intendants of the houses. As they progressed up the scale from provincial house to the major cities, ballet directors were hired and fired on a yearly basis. Even today, promising companies are disbanded because the opera director leaves, an odd situation, but the accepted one, throughout Germany.

Below: Marcia Haydée and Richard Cragun in John Cranko's Romeo and Juliet.

In Berlin Tatiana Gsovsky had organized a large company and created a large repertoire: a mixture of the classical and expressionist styles in which she had been trained. There were also several guest ballet masters, including Anthony Tudor, who produced both *Giselle* and his own *Gala Performance*, but the only period of any length which produced notable works was the three years of Kenneth Macmillan's directorship, although even he had problems coping with the opera house mentality. Macmillan created large-scale versions of *Swan Lake* and *The Sleeping Beauty*, and mounted his own earlier work, *Solitaire*. From this time we also have *Concerto*, to Shostakovitch's Second Piano Concerto, with its beautiful lyric *pas de deux* to the second movement, as well as the one-act *Anastasia*. Set to Martinu's *Fantaisies Symphonique*, this became the third act of the full-length version given by the Royal Ballet in 1971. It gave another great dramatic role to his ballerina, Lynn Seymour, who had joined him in Berlin.

Lynn Seymour became director of the ballet in Munich in 1978, a company which has enjoyed a long and checkered history. In 1795 the Viganos had appeared there in *La Fille Mal Gardée* and been accused of obscenity, and Lucile Grahn was ballet mistress of the company from 1869 to 1875. A street was named in her memory – for her charitable works as well as for the ballet. Several important productions were given in this house immediately after the war and during the 1950s Alan Carter produced the first German versions of Benjamin Britten's *Prince of the Pagodas* and Hans Werner Henze's *Ondine*.

Since that time several directors have come and gone. They included, for a brief interim period, John Cranko, who combined it with his work in Stuttgart. The present-day company has strong dancers led by the German ballerina Konstanze Vernon, who also directs the ballet school, and it includes such dancers as the outstanding Japanese, Hideo Fukagawa. The repertoire is as eclectic as ever, but centers around the classics and the great works of Cranko.

It was a production of *The Prince of the Pagodas* which took John Cranko to Stuttgart and gave Germany its first, indeed only, company of international stature. Stuttgart had had a notable background in ballet history, having been the home of Noverre, but apart from a brief stay by Marie Taglioni and her father, nothing of great importance had happened since then. Nicholas Beriosoff, father of Svetlana Beriosova, worked in Stuttgart for two years from 1958 and mounted many of the classics. This base gave Cranko something to work on when he accepted the invitation to take over the direction of the company in 1961.

The invitation from the Intendant, Walter Erich Schäfer, to produce *The Prince of the Pagodas* which Cranko had originally made for the Royal Ballet in 1957, came at the right moment for him. His last productions in London, *Antigone* for the Royal Ballet and the revue *New Cranks*, had not lived up to public expectancy.

Once in Stuttgart Cranko set about creating a team around him and he was particularly fortunate to find Marcia Haydée, a Brazilian ballerina, who became his inspiration, just as Seymour was to Macmillan and Fonteyn to Ashton. Haydée developed as a brilliant dramatic ballerina, the perfect expression of Cranko's particular, athletic version of classicism. She could reflect his brilliant character-izations and bring a natural, free-flowing virtuosity to his *pas de deux* full of difficult and inventive lifts. She found her perfect partner in Richard Cragun, a brilliant technician with a totally charming stage manner.

The strength of the team Cranko gathered around him is evident from the way the company has continued after his untimely death in 1973. Following a brief interim period under Glen Tetley, which inspired him to produce *Greening*, the company is now directed by Marcia Haydée. The Cranko tradition is kept alive in a positive way and the school he founded (for he had followed the example set by Ninette de Valois) is now one of the most important in Germany.

Cranko also encouraged John Neumeier, a dancer in his company, to develop his choreography and within a very short time to take over the direction of the Frankfurt Ballet. Neumeier is now regarded by some as the most important 'German' choreog-rapher, although he was in fact born in Milwaukee and trained at the Royal Ballet School. The British connection was strengthened by the fact that one of his earliest choreographies was *Frontiers* for the Scottish Ballet in 1969, the year he took over Frankfurt. He soon created two full-length works – *Romeo and Juliet*, which he recreated for the Royal Danish Ballet as well as his own Hamburg Ballet, and *The Nutcracker* in a particularly original version.

Since then he has concentrated on producing his own, often controversial, versions of other classics as well as a stream of works which give much greater importance to the literary idea than to the steps. It is refreshing to find such an intelligence working in the ballet, but saddening that these ideas are not always translated successfully into dance. Following in the Cranko tradition Neumeier has formed a closely knit family of dancers and teachers to communicate his ideas. The emphasis is on expression rather than technique and the stars are very much the first among equals.

Alfonso Cata had made a very valiant effort to create a company based on the Balanchine repertoire as well as the classics in Frankfurt following Neumeier's departure. This small company danced particularly fine productions of ballets such as *Four Temperaments* and *Serenade*, but sadly it was disbanded when there was a change of opera direction.

The high point of the classic ballet seems now to have almost passed its peak in Germany and the trend appears to be toward smaller, modern-based companies. Berlin remains a large-scale company with a constant stream of visiting choreog-raphers, and the company in Dusseldorf under Erich Walter is marking time choreographically. In the smaller towns which once had classical companies, such as Mannheim, there are now only modern companies and a *corps de ballet* to supply the needs of opera for human scenery and of operetta for waltzes.

The trend back to modern dance followed the change in direction in Cologne,

Above: Marcia Haydée and Richard Cragun in Kenneth Macmillan's Requiem, *created for the Stuttgart company in memory of John Cranko.*

Left: The Stuttgart Ballet have a program to encourage new choreographers, such as Patrice Montagnon who created Innere Not.

where a moderately successful classical company was disbanded and at the same time a prosperous Summer Academy, largely orientated toward modern dance, was set up. Tanz Forum Cologne, as the company is now known, is one of the three major modern companies in Germany and has provided an outlet for both American and British modern choreographers, such as Christopher Bruce whose work is also represented in Munich.

In 1969 the winner of the Choreographic Prize at the Cologne Summer Academy was Pina Bausch. A product of the Essen School, she is now director of the Wuppertal company and a leading figure of the modern revival, with dances such as *The Rite of Spring*, created in 1975.

The Dutch National Ballet based in Amsterdam has grown out of two other classical companies which merged under the joint direction of their respective founders, Sonia Gaskell and Masche ter Weeme, in 1961. Eventually Miss Gaskell assumed direction, but the company is now in the hands of the choreographer Rudi van Dantzig. One of the largest companies in the world, it has only since that time acquired a definite character, largely through van Dantzig's works in the modern classical mold. They are usually intensely personal, deriving from childhood experience, such as *Monument for a Dead Boy*, and deeply influenced by the stern Dutch Calvinist tradition.

Although in recent years the repertoire has leaned more heavily on such works and on those of Toer van Schayk, also a noted designer, the classics are regularly produced and the company boasts such notable dancers as Alexandra Radius and Han Ebbelaar. Together with Hans van Manen and Benjamin Harkavy they were both founder members of Netherlands Dans Theater. This company, now one of the most important modern dance companies in the world, is one of inestimable importance to the growth of modern dance in Europe.

From the outset the aim was to produce new choreography and they succeeded. In the early years they averaged 10 new productions a year and that number grew to something like 16. The quality was uniformly stimulating, although there was room for only a few of these works in the permanent repertoire.

The company was, and is, classically based and it is only in recent years that classes in modern technique have been given regularly. The repertoire reflected this with a well-balanced mixture of classical and modern works. Hans van Manen, though a classical dancer, soon blended the two into his own particular style, just as Glen Tetley, a modern dancer, absorbed the classical technique after his arrival in 1962 as dancer and choreographer. Both have now grown into choreographers of world standing with works found in many repertoires.

Below: Nederlands Dans Theater in Hans van Manen's Grosse Fuge.

Above: Two scenes from Nils Christe's **Miniatures** *with Arlette van Boven, top left, one of Nederlands Dans Theater's most outstanding dancers. Christe has produced several original works including a comedy piece,* **Tofuba,** *and* **Glissando,** *inspired by ice skating.*

The company has been particularly important in introducing American choreographers to Europe with varying degrees of success. John Butler produced *Carmina Burana*, the company's keynote ballet for many years, and Glen Tetley produced his masterwork, *Pierrot Lunaire*. Louis Falco produced provocative and amusing works, which led the company up a cul-de-sac for some seasons, but they are now back firmly on the main road of creativity.

The company is now directed by Jiri Kylian, a product of both the Royal Ballet School and Cranko's Stuttgart company. His choreography, in a muted, neo-classical style, is the basis of the repertoire, but, as ever, new choreographers are being encouraged. Foremost among these is Nils Christe, a dancer with the company, unique for his independent style, his sense of humor and the invention in his themes and movements.

Although Jiri Kylian's *La Cathédrale Engloutie* has been produced for the Ballet of Flanders in Antwerp, there is little true modern activity in Belgium. For most people interested in dance, Belgium means Béjart. The growth of the Béjart phenomenon amuses, angers and intrigues many people in the world of the classical ballet. His many advantages, not least of all the way he has widened the audience for ballet, appear to have too many disadvantages to counterbalance them. The two other companies in Belgium, the Ballet of Flanders in Antwerp and the Ballet of Wallonie in Charleroi, pale into insignificance compared with the Ballet of the Twentieth Century formed by Maurice Béjart in Brussels in 1960.

Maurice Béjart was born in Marseilles and studied ballet there and in Paris and London with such notable teachers as Egorova and Volkova, making his debut as a dancer in 1945. He danced with various groups and companies, including those of Petit and Charrat, as well as with the Royal Swedish Ballet. In 1953 he formed his first company, eventually called the Ballets de l'Etoile and finally the Ballet de Maurice Béjart for which he created the first works such as *Symphonie pour un homme seul*, for which he was to become famous, if not infamous.

It was this group which combined in 1959 with the Janine Charrat company and Britain's Western Theatre Ballet to create *The Rite of Spring* in Brussels. From the success of this season grew the Ballet of the Twentieth Century based at the Théâtre de la Monnaie.

Since that time the company has aquired a special place in ballet, appealing to a large popular audience wherever it has appeared. It has toured the world, usually playing to mass audiences in sports stadiums and arenas in place of the more usual theaters. Béjart's spectacles often appear more at home in these large open spaces. Confined within a proscenium arch they often lose their effect and the weakness of the actual choreography becomes more apparent.

By some happy chance Béjart has always managed to mirror the moment with his choice of theme, striking a particularly fruitful seam with his works based on oriental mysticism, such as *Bhakti*. His large-scale symphonic works, such as *Ninth Symphony*, stress a simplistic view of humanity, as does his reworking of *The Firebird* which emerged as the spirit of revolution.

His use of modern music, particularly works by Boulez and Stockhausen, has been

Above: Kevin Haigen, François Klaus and Magali Messac in John Neumeier's Mahler 4th.

Right: The Dutch National Ballet with Rudolf Nureyev in Rudi van Dantzig's About a Dark House.

an important popularizer of these difficult works and there is no denying his brilliance as a master of stagecraft and effect. He can produce simple, striking tableaux of exceptional potency. He is the master of the poster effect, which is perhaps one of the reasons more serious ballet viewers do not find him satisfying.

An offshoot of his oriental interests has been MUDRA, his school and studio for developing theater; part dance school, part philosophical experience. The Béjart style is firmly based on the classical technique and he has had a particularly good eye for choosing dancers to interpret his works, including ballerinas such as Tania Bari, Maina Gielgud and, briefly, Suzanne Farrell. Male dancers, who play an even greater part in the success of his ballets, have included Paolo Bortoluzzi and Jorge Donn.

His ballets are not much performed by other companies and he rarely creates for them. An exception has been the Paris Opéra for which he created Berlioz' *Damnation of Faust* as well as Stravinsky's *Renard* and *The Firebird*.

When Rolf Liebermann assumed direction of the Opéra he introduced works by George Balanchine, who had created *Le Palais de Cristal* there in 1947. Under the same title as the Bizet music, *Symphony in C*, it is now one of the most exciting works in the international repertoire. Balanchine has continued to produce ballets for the company up to the present and in 1975 collaborated with it to arrange the Ravel Festival in New York. Jerome Robbins contributed works to this program as well. A similar cultural exchange has taken place between the Opéra and the Bolshoi Ballet in Moscow. The results have not been artistically admirable, but they did bring Grigoriev's *Ivan the Terrible* into the West.

Right: The Paris Opéra has produced
many fine male dancers in recent years,
such as Michael Denard, Patrice Bart,
Jacques Namont, left, and most recently
Patrick Dupont.

Below: Peter Schaufuss with Roland
Petit as Dr Coppelius in Petit's Coppelia.

The ballet of France still revolves around the Opéra, but there have been deliberate attempts by the Ministry of Culture to organize regional companies in recent years, based on the various Maisons de la Culture which were set up as art complexes to house exhibitions, concerts and theater. The only one of these to make any great impact has been the Ballet Théâtre Contemporain originally founded in Amiens in 1968. It had a very definite, and admirable, policy of presenting only new works with music created in this century and designed by a wide range of modern artists. In spite of the choreographic efforts of Françoise Adret and Michel Descombey it became more noted for its outstanding décors, and before its latest change of base (to Nancy) it provided an outlet for the avant-garde American choreographers Louis Falco and Jennifer Muller following their period with Netherlands Dans Theater.

Rosella Hightower, director designate at the Paris Opéra, has made various attempts to form companies along the Riviera using her large school in Cannes as a base, but so far none has become permanent. Roland Petit, however, has had considerably more success. Following the demise of his various companies in the 1950s, which was a particularly productive time for him, he choreographed many films, including *Daddy Long Legs* and *Hans Christian Andersen*, as well as shows. He revived the great days of the Casino de Paris for his wife Zizi Jeanmaire and also went on to produce ballets for the Paris Opéra as well as less successful works for Margot Fonteyn and Rudolf Nureyev in London (*Pelléas and Melisande*) and the National Ballet of Canada. If not as successful choreographically they still showed his supreme mastery of stagecraft and production, a talent he used to the full with the Marseilles Ballet which he has directed since 1972. There he has created a company with a strong cohesive style and has also managed to introduce brilliant guests such as Mikhail Baryshnikov and Peter Schaufuss, in ballets such as *The Queen of Spades*, *The Bat* and *Coppelia*.

In spite of an adventurous air in France, most recent development has been in the field of the classic dance and as yet there is no established modern dance company. The Opéra promotes a modern group directed by Carolyn Carlson which has given provocative programs by Merce Cunningham. Jacques Garnier's Théâtre du Silence presents productions in a mixture of styles of which the *coup de théâtre* is the most obvious.

Italy has yet to break back into the mainstream of ballet in a creative way and the many excellent dancers produced there leave if they wish to develop. The great ballerina Carla Fracci has made many attempts to found companies, but they end as little more than backing groups for her performances in established classics during the summer season. Companies persist, attached to most of the opera houses, but the political and bureaucratic climate is not conducive to growth and, with the notable exceptions of some productions by Rudolf Nureyev at La Scala, Milan (*The Sleeping Beauty*, for example), no important works have been produced. The Rome Opera lost its ballerina, Elisabetta Terabust, first to the Roland Petit Company and lately to London Festival Ballet; Paolo Bortoluzzi has made most of his outstanding career away from his company in Milan.

Above: Maina Gielgud, who made her name with Maurice Béjart but later developed as a classical ballerina, with Germinal Casado in Béjart's Bhakti.

Opposite: Ballet Théâtre Contemporain in Hopop.

As with other countries so important to the birth of ballet, Austria today has no tradition of its own. The particularly well-known Opera House has considerable funds and so Vienna can attract international choreographers with ease, such as John Neumeier who created his own version of the Richard Strauss work, *Legend of Joseph*.

Sweden in recent years has fared a little better and can boast thriving classical companies in Stockholm and Gothenburg as well as an active modern dance scene led by Birgit Cullberg. Although she has worked largely with the classical technique in ballets such as *Miss Julie*, created in 1950 and based on the Strindberg play, she has recently attempted to adapt this style into a more consciously modern look. Her subjects have increasingly political overtones and are often turgidly stated, but she has played an important part in the statement of Swedish themes on the dance stage.

At the Royal Swedish Ballet there is an enormous repertoire representing the best of recent choreography. There has been little original creation for the company, the exception being Nureyev's *The Nutcracker*, in 1967, but they regularly perform works by Cranko (*Eugene Onegin*), Macmillan (*Romeo and Juliet*), Ashton (*La Fille Mal Gardée*) and Robbins (*Les Noces*). Nureyev's period of work there was particularly difficult and highlighted the problems of the company – an inbred laziness due perhaps to job security and excellent working conditions. This has held back what could be a major world company. The facilities available are second to none and the native talent is among the best in Europe. The company is currently producing excellent male dancers through their own school, a sure sign of strength.

In Gothenburg the ballet has an important reputation largely through publicity given to the work there by the Danish ballerina Elsa Marianne von Rosen with ballets such as *Napoli* and *La Sylphide*. It is now directed by the young Swede, Ulf Gadd, a particularly productive choreographer. Always provocative, his ballets have included a controversial *Sleeping Beauty* for the Royal Swedish Ballet and *The Miraculous Mandarin* to the Bartok score which has been produced in Berlin and New York.

The Danish tradition is almost completely male and this continues to be its strength today. Although the company experienced some unsettled direction in the 1950s and early 1960s the strong tradition of Bournonville continued and in fact the

Right: Switzerland at last has a Swiss choreographer, Heinz Spoerhli of Basle, in charge of one of its several companies. His most recent full-length ballet was Ondine *with Maria Guerrero, Chris Jensen and Harman Tromp.*

Below: The Royal Danish Ballet maintain their traditional repertoire, but in recent years they have performed controversial modern ballets such as The Triumph of Death *by Flemming Flindt, seen below, as well as works by John Neumeier, Murray Louis and, bottom left,* Septet Extra *by Hans van Manen.*

company realized, perhaps a little late, that they should actively encourage other companies to produce his works. They had always been cut off and through their connection with the Royal Theater which committed them to subscription performances, a problem German companies in particular experience today, the time available for foreign tours was severely limited. Even up to today they rarely travel abroad, but at least small groups of dancers tour in their long holidays. In 1979, the centenary of Bournonville's death, a particularly ambitious tour took place during which three of the great Danish dancers of today took part: Peter Martins, Niels Kehlet and Peter Schaufuss, together with some of the brilliant young dancers, such as Ib Andersen, which the Royal Danish Ballet School still produces.

The emphasis is still strongly on male dancing and it is sad that there is no Danish ballerina in the mold of Margarethe Schanne, a great Sylphide, or Mona Vangsaae, creator of Frederick Ashton's Juliet and a host of other important dramatic roles. The company has been directed by great male dancers such as Frank Schaufuss, Niels Bjorn Larsen, Flemming Flindt and Henning Kronstam. Flindt took the company through its most controversial period and produced a stream of his own highly idiosyncratic works, such as *The Lesson* and *The Young Man Must Marry*, both based on plays by Ionesco, and *The Triumph of Death*.

The company in Oslo, Norway, belongs to no particular tradition and does not have any special connection with Denmark or even Sweden other than sharing a few dancers. The repertoire is international, and ballet master, Poul Gnatt, Danish and the director, Brenda Last, a product of the Royal Ballet. As with Denmark there is little modern dance activity other than experiments in modern classical dance.

With the arrival of the classic tradition now established in most European countries, it cannot be long before modern dance makes a similar breakthrough.

America

The dance scene in America today is still dominated by the two large classical companies, New York City Ballet and American Ballet Theater, the latter enjoying a period of revival largely due to the presence of guest stars such as Natalia Makarova and Mikhail Baryshnikov. It has, however, produced a star ballerina of its own in Cynthia Gregory and also includes such young dancers as Gelsey Kirkland, a product of Mr Balanchine's company, and Leslie Browne and George de la Pena, who have made highly acclaimed performances on film in *The Turning Point* and *Nijinsky*. The repertoire is based on large-scale popular works such as *Giselle* and *The Nutcracker*, although Mary Skeaping's production of *The Sleeping Beauty* proved unsuccessful; the American dancers could not catch her particularly European style. Anthony Tudor has produced ballets such as *Leaves are Fading . . .*, and from the modern dance

Left: Gelsey Kirkland and Charles Ward in Anthony Tudor's Leaves are Fading . . . *for American Ballet Theater.*

Right: Mikhail Baryshnikov in the solo, Vestris, *created to show off his spectacular technique by Leonide Jacobsen while he was still with the Kirov Ballet.*

world Alvin Ailey has created *The River* and Twyla Tharp *Push Comes to Shove* for Baryshnikov. The company has no permanent home and spends much of its life on tour. It has not produced a choreographer of its own other than Denis Nahat who created ballets such as *Mendelssohn Symphony*, but left to found and direct the Cleveland Ballet.

The New York City Ballet, still firmly under the direction of George Balanchine, is safely installed in its own theater as part of the Lincoln Center, and the School of American Ballet, having the pick of young dancers from across the continent, produces an outstanding batch of prospective company members every year. The school faculty includes such eminent names as Danilova, for many years a close colleague of Mr B, as he is affectionately known throughout the ballet world. Much of

Above: Mikhail Baryshnikov in Other Dances *created for him and Natalia Makarova by Jerome Robbins. Set to a waltz and four mazurkas by Chopin, they are related to his* Dances at a Gathering – *hence the title.*

the teaching of the boys is in the hands of Stanley Williams, for many years a dancer with the Royal Danish Ballet. The Danish connection has been very strong in recent years with Peter Martins, the epitome of the *danseur noble* at the head of the company alongside the all-American Jacques d'Amboise and Edward Villella. He was joined by Helgi Tomassen, Peter Schaufuss (briefly), and Adam Luders. Mr Balanchine's powers are undiminished and he continues to produce a stream of ballets inspired by his ballerinas, with whom he has a special affinity. In his early years male dancing did not interest him, but recently he has made use of the exceptional talent available. However, his best works center around his ideal – the long-legged ballerinas such as Suzanne Farrell, Kay Mazzo, Gelsey Kirkland and his latest discovery, Merrill Ashley.

Left: The Alvin Ailey Company in the opening section of Ailey's Revelations.

Left: Tent *by Alwin Nikolais.*

Right: Rudolf Nureyev in Paul Taylor's Aureole.

Following his return to ballet with *Dances at a Gathering*, Jerome Robbins has produced an eclectic series of works with no apparent common theme, each being successful in its own right. He has pursued deeper themes, such as in *The Dybbuk*, yet he seems more at home in lighter, pure dance works. The repertoire still centers around these two choreographers although recently Peter Martins has started to choreograph, his first very successful effort being *Calcium Light* to music by the American composer Charles Ives.

The Joffrey Ballet is perhaps the best example of the difficulties facing smaller classical companies in the struggle for survival. That it does exist at all is due to the dogged persistence of its founder, Robert Joffrey, who kept his group together through the most difficult times, including the withdrawal of finance by Rebekah Harkness (who eventually used, and lost, most of it on her own venture, The Harkness Ballet). The company originally relied heavily on the choreographic talents of Gerald Arpino and he still produces at least one ballet a season with the same

Above: Suzanne Farrell and Peter Martins in Balanchine's Chaconne.

Left: Farrell and Martins in the Diamonds pas de deux *from Balanchine's full-evening work,* Jewels.

complete facility. His talent lies in being able to produce the ballet of the moment, but he has yet to produce one of lasting quality. His ballets create momentary interest through effect, but are not at all satisfying as dance.

To give the repertoire substance the company has, since 1969, mounted not only a large number of Diaghilev ballets (*Petrouchka*, *The Three-Cornered Hat* and *Parade*), but also important works by Frederick Ashton which were not hitherto represented in the American repertoire. The company danced one ballet by Alvin Ailey (*Feast of Ashes*) in 1962, one of the earliest collaborations between the modern and classical schools. Martha Graham and George Balanchine had collaborated with *Episodes* in 1959, but in reality they had shared a stage and composer (Webern) rather than created together. In 1973 Joffrey commissioned a work from Twyla Tharp, *Deuce Coupe*, which gave them one of their greatest successes and had wider implications in the world of dance.

Tharp's involvement has become a significant creative addition to the classical

Below: The Joffrey Ballet in Arpino's Drums, Dreams and Banjos.

ballet. Belonging to no firm modern school, although she studied with Cunningham and danced with the Paul Taylor company, Tharp has evolved a highly idiosyncratic style which seems to sit naturally on classical dancers and opens up new possibilities for them. The style is outwardly flip and throwaway, but the structure, particularly the footwork, is precise. The effect is casual, but the dances are profoundly musical. The overall impact is invariably appealing, though cerebral and intense. Through her own sometimes frenetic dance style (Tharp always seems busy) with its abrupt changes of tempo or direction, she creates dances which literally make audiences sit up and look. Popular social dance steps – she has used popular music ranging from Bix Beiderbecke to the Beach Boys – are shown in a new context and with a new significance. Since the success of *Deuce Coupe*, which also had a new style of decor created onstage during the dances by graffiti artists from the New York Subway, she has gone on to make further works for Joffrey and American Ballet Theater, as well as choreographing the film version of *Hair*.

Other small classical companies have come and gone, but they are not able to thrive like the small modern companies. Classical dance takes more organization and more established facilities. It cannot be danced in the lofts, public spaces or tiny theaters which house the myriad modern dance groups. In New York, Eliot Feld has attempted to keep a group going, but apart from the problems facing any company, save New York City Ballet, of living on the works of one choreographer, tours have been interspersed with extensive layoffs while Feld has mounted his ballets, such as *Harbinger* and *At Midnight*, elsewhere.

Right: Mikhail Baryshnikov in Twyla Tharp's Push Comes to Shove.

Below: Twyla Tharp and her company.

The fate of the Harkness Ballet, with its seemingly unlimited funds, emphasizes these problems. Talented dancers performing a lightweight repertoire, heavily biased toward the ideas of the moment and without serious choreographic talent, simply cannot keep going. It gave an outlet to choreographers such as Brian MacDonald and Alvin Ailey, but did not find a permanent place on the American dance scene.

In spite of obvious reasons why it should find a permanent place, the Harlem Ballet is not without its difficulties. This company grew out of the teaching activities in Harlem of Arthur Mitchell, one of Mr Balanchine's great dancers, at the time of the death of Martin Luther King in 1968. The school is now of gigantic size and the company, which gave its first performance in 1970, has grown to considerable stature. It is still a classical company and dances many works by Balanchine, but there are inevitable pressures for it to present works with a more ethnic content. This is contrary to Mitchell's initial concept since he wanted an outlet for black American classical dancers, but a more popular repertoire may be forced on him simply to bring in audiences. In Europe, particularly in Spoleto and London, they have had enormous success, but this does not automatically guarantee a steady existence at home. The dancers cope magnificently with the demands of a repertoire which can range from *Concerto Barocco* by Balanchine to a classic *pas de deux* to a piece set to Negro spirituals, but in the end one style inevitably suffers.

There is a very strong dance program in most universities across America, unlike in Europe where the idea of a degree in dance still sounds odd. These courses

Below: Laura Brown and Paul Russell of the Harlem Ballet in Le Corsaire.

Above: Susan Lovelle as Eve, Homer Bryant as Adam and Mel Tomlinson as the Snake in Harlem Ballet's Manifestations.

embrace both modern and classical dance and have been very important in the tremendous growth in recent years of regional ballet across America. Most large cities have a company of some sort, many having a completely professional one, although some employ professional principals only, the *corps de ballet* being made up of the students. Modern dance companies spend periods as 'dancers in residence' with universities and many famous names from the past of the classical ballet are found at the head of dance departments.

Pittsburgh maintains a large company with an equally large repertoire, made up mostly of their own versions of the classics, balanced by short works from the international repertoire as well as a few locally-created ones. The company is headed by Dagmar Kessler, one of the few American ballerinas permanently based outside New York. Her early training was in Pennsylvania which now boasts one of the most successful regional companies in every sense. They have relied heavily on the Balanchine repertoire, which is generously made available through both government and private funding. To this the company has added works by its associate artistic director, Benjamin Harkavy, a more noted teacher and coach than choreographer, John Butler and Lar Lubovitch, a modern choreographer who has produced many works with a strongly classical flavor. Harkavy's fellow founder of Nederlands Dans Theater, Hans van Manen, is also represented with ballets such as *Grosse Fuge*. The company gives regular New York performances in the Brooklyn Academy of Music, which is in effect their New York base, and enjoys a high critical reputation.

Other companies of note are found in Boston, Los Angeles (under the direction of John Clifford, a talented performer) and San Francisco, where Michael Smuin is building a new strong company. In Chicago, which at the time of Ruth Page's Opera Ballet appeared to be putting down firm roots, classical ballet activity is now represented by a star-studded festival each year. In Seattle Kent Stowell, a former principal dancer of the New York City Ballet, and his wife, Francia Russell, one of the most talented producers of Balanchine's ballets, are organizing both school and company, while in Houston Ben Stevenson, a former dancer with London Festival Ballet, is building up the company there and has introduced ballets by Barry Moreland (*The Prodigal Son* in ragtime) to complement those by resident choreographer James Clouser. Stevenson has worked extensively in America, but he has been only associated with ill-fated ventures such as the Chicago Ballet and the National Ballet which was based on Washington. His efforts there with Frederic Franklin looked, for a time, as though they would be successful, but the large repertoire of full-length classics did not find an audience and eventually they were forced to close through the inevitable lack of funds.

Established modern dancers, too, have difficulty keeping their companies together for any length of time and either have prolonged periods of layoff or, if fortunate, find a residency at a university. Alvin Ailey was lucky to become associated with the City Center in New York which secured him a base, but although he has had a policy of presenting the best of American modern dance, the company appear to have lost impetus recently and programs rely increasingly on well-tried formulae. They invariably close with *Revelations* which he choreographed to a set of Negro spirituals. No other dance has reached the popularity of this one and it is suffering seriously from over-exposure; the applause it brings overshadows the weakness of the rest of the repertoire.

Below: Clive Thomson with the Alvin Ailey company in Blues Suite.

Right: The Alvin Nikolais Company in the Mantis section of Imago.

Above: Christopher Aponte of the Harkness Ballet.

Alwin Nikolais is still a force in modern dance and has recently made more use of dancers than before. He was always a man more interested in presentation and total theater rather than dance as such, and his initial impact and lasting influence lie in his startlingly inventive use of lighting effects, materials and costumes. Dancers rarely looked like dancers, but were cocooned in tubes of gauze or swathed in chiffon. Their limbs were extended outward and upward with ribbons and banners while their bodies were distorted with wire frameworks. The movement was not human movement. Dancers were reduced to part of the moving whole of the production, often doing nothing more than repetitive, machine-like jerkings. The effect, though at the cost of totally depersonalizing the dancers, was stunning and it is from these productions that many other producers, particularly in the legitimate theater, have drawn inspiration.

Nikolais' chief pupil and dancer, Murray Louis, who was the most brilliant exponent of the nervous twitching and jerky actions which comprised Nikolais' choreography for a great part of his career, has now emerged as a choreographer in his own right. He has largely used his own dance talent plus a quirky sense of humor, but has recently broadened his style through work with classical dancers such as those of the Royal Danish Ballet as well as Rudolf Nureyev. The Nikolais style, which uses the body in a totally plastic way, transforming it into a myriad of other shapes and forms, has been taken to a peak of manic invention by the dance group Pilobus Dance Theater. Their invention reaches zany heights, but is unsatisfying artistically after more than one viewing. One can admire the invention, but rarely be moved by it.

Alwin Nikolais is one of the small group of dancers and choreographers who began to take over from the founders of mainstream modern dance, the innovators who created systems and schools, as they gradually passed from the scene in the 1950s. Only Martha Graham is still active, as the presiding genius of her own company, and it is her pupils and collaborators who formed the main part of that group, which included her ex-husband, Erick Hawkins, ex-dancers, Merce Cunningham and Paul Taylor, together with the joker-in-the-pack, James Waring, who seemed to have been influenced by everyone. In his turn, before his sudden death in 1975, he influenced almost everyone else.

Merce Cunningham

Merce Cunningham is the central link between the originators of modern dance and the present generation of free dancers. He is still the most important innovator in the field and has opened up endless possibilities for young choreographers, not only those who have grown from his own group.

Cunningham brings together all the elements ideal for a perfect dance performance and then adds one – dance as its own subject matter. This startlingly simply concept is Cunningham's chief contribution to the development of dance. He rejects the necessity for subject matter whether it be literary or psychological. He rejects the need for his dances, and therefore all others, to be wed to music. His dances literally stand on their own two feet. This has been the most basic challenge to the concept of dance, either classical or modern. Dance was freed from its dependence on musical structure. Music is something which, if used at all, just happens at the same time as the dance.

Below: Barbara Lloyd and Merce Cunningham in Rainforest, *made in 1968 with music by David Tudor and décor by Andy Warhol.*

Born in Centralia, Washington State, in 1909, Cunningham received his early training at the Cornish School of Fine and Applied Arts in Seattle. Here, in the late 1930s, at much the same time as he started to work with Martha Graham, he met John Cage. Cage, avant-garde musician extraordinary, was a major influence throughout his career and instrumental in the formulation of the idea of divorcing dance from dependence on the rhythmical impulse of music.

After joining Martha Graham in 1939, only the second man in her company, Cunningham danced in such important works as *El Penitente, Letter to the World* and *Appalachian Spring.* Expressively and technically he was a great performer in the Graham mold and might well have settled down to become an interpreter of her works. But by 1942, just two years after joining her, he was already creating his own dances, first with Jean Erdman and Nina Fonaroff, and then in 1942 a solo, *Totem Ancestor,* which set a pattern for the future. In collaboration with John Cage he gave a series of solo concerts across America and also created a work for the Ballet Society, forerunner of New York City Ballet, in 1947.

His interest in the possibility of movement as such and the creation of dances by chance was given greater expression when he formed his own company in 1953 and created *Suite by Chance.* Like John Cage, Cunningham wanted to completely overturn any preconceived ideas the audience might have about dance and music. In *Dime a Dance,* that same year, the order of the separate sections of the work was determined by the audience. Members were invited to pay a dime to pick a card from a pack to give the sequence of dances.

Chance, to Cunningham, is a carefully guarded and, indeed, calculated method, which may seem a contradiction in terms. He plans in great detail what elements are in a ballet and then introduces the element of chance as a joker in the pack. From the simplest of beginnings, tossing a coin to determine a sequence, he developed procedures of great complexity.

In these early days chance played a part in the composition of the work, either dance or music, but afterward it became formalized during performance. From this developed the idea of 'open form' where the works were in a state of constant change from performance to performance. In many respects *Dime a Dance* bridges both these concepts, having elements of chance in the composition and 'open form' in the arrangement of the performance. From 'open form,' which can be seen in such works as *Canfield* and *Landrover,* there developed the further concept of 'events.'

'Events' to some extent derived from the greater number of performances, to use the traditional term, which were given in places other than the theater. The vast growth of modern dance in universities and colleges, particularly in America, meant that many performances were taking place in gymnasiums, museums, assembly halls or other public places, which led to the total breakdown of the theatrical concept. The audience, too, was new and Cunningham, like other modern dancers, found a keen following of young people, particularly students.

Into these events Cunningham poured his total experience. His complete repertoire of structured and unstructured dances was to be unravelled and recreated in new forms. Pieces from several different works were given at the same time, with a minimum of rehearsal, perhaps only on the day of performance. Old works were given new views. Audiences and dancers alike were given a revitalized idea of works they had hitherto accepted.

Cunningham has been an influential teacher, though his technique is transparent. The dancers he has produced are virtuosos, but with an almost indefinable virtuosity. They build infinitely complex dances into their bodies, they have an intellectual stature to cope with the demands of the open form performances.

Cunningham continues to inspire and to recreate. His visionary processes have long since surpassed any conceivable description as choreography. The word is altogether too limiting. He redefined choreography, and he redefined dancing.

Paul Taylor danced with Merce Cunningham's company in 1953 and made his first choreographies in 1955. He danced with the Martha Graham company and created the role of Aegisthus in *Clytemnestra*, at the same time continuing his choreographic experiments such as *Epic* (1957), set to recorded telephone time signals and with lighting by Robert Rauschenberg, who designed many of his future dances. Taylor is a big man with a broad expansive outlook. This geniality breaks through even in his most serious works, and his immediate appeal was that, unlike so many experimenters and innovators, he always had an infectious sense of humor and a joyousness which came through either in pure dance (*Aureole* for instance) or in his black, black comedies. *Aureole* was one of the first modern works created for a modern company to be taken into the repertoire of a classical company, the Royal Danish Ballet, and it has now been extensively performed at the Paris Opéra. Rudolf Nureyev includes it in his Nureyev and Friends programs, and has danced as a member of Taylor's company.

As with so many modern creators the dance movement which Taylor has evolved is

Below: London Contemporary Dance Theatre in Paul Taylor's Three Epitaphs, *set to American folk music uncertainly played by brass band. The glittering costumes are by Robert Rauschenberg.*

entirely his own, and just as the Graham style in the main roles seemed weaker when not danced by Graham herself, so Taylor's occasionally lacks the personality of its begetter. His themes, however, are usually strong and full of decadent jokes. In *Churchyard* the jolly cavorting peasants acquire very odd bumps and growths under their tights as the dance progresses to its gruesome end and in *Agathe's Tale* the pure heroine not only gets involved in an orgy with Satan and Pan, but also manages to involve the Unicorn which is supposed to be protecting her virginity. Taylor built up an excellent team of dancers which included the beautiful Bettie de Jong, Carolyn Adams and Dan Wagoner, who now has his own dance group.

The complex relationships and inter-relationships in the world of modern dance are infinitely more difficult to unravel than those of the classical ballet. There are almost as many choreographers as there are dancers and the groups they draw around them form and reform constantly. This was true throughout the 1950s and 1960s and the pace of change is now quickening. Without preparing an exhaustive list of dancers it is almost impossible to do justice to everyone.

Below: Paul Taylor's company in his Piece Period. *The music by Telemann, Vivaldi, Scarlatti and others is authentic, but the actions completely deflate period attitudes.*

Of the 1950s generation Anna Sokolow had a lasting influence with works such as *Rooms*, successfully staged in London as one of the early productions by the reformed Ballet Rambert. Paul Sanasardo was one of the original dancers in it and he began producing works in the early 1960s as well as talented pupils, such as Manuel Alum, who became associate choreographer with Sanasardo's group. At much the same time Louis Falco was making a great impression as a dancer with the José Limón company. In 1968 he created *Huescape*, one of his most successful works, revived for Nederlands Dans Theater during his time of influence there. His dances are always strongly designed and he has built up a close relationship with a group of avant-garde artists including Marisol and William Katz. One of his close colleagues, the dancer Jennifer Muller who has developed as a choreographer, played an important part in mounting works of José Limón for other companies such as American Ballet Theater. Limón's *The Moor's Pavane*, the story of Othello reduced to its barest essentials as a *pas de quatre*, has slowly entered the international repertoire. Muller herself has created curious pieces of theater for Nederlands Dans Theater (*Strangers* and *American Beauty Rose*) as well as for Ballet Théâtre Contemporain.

Above: Louis Falco and Jennifer Muller in Falco's The Sleepers.

Top right: Senta Driver and her group creating Crowd.

Bottom right: Douglas Dunn, a brilliant dancer with Twyla Tharp and other companies, rehearsing.

Kei Takei, a protégé of Anna Sokolow, and her group in After Lunch, *1975.*

The Limón influence, through the Doris Humphrey connection, is also felt today through pupils such as Ann Halprin, who have become persuasive teachers themselves. In many ways the Humphrey ethic is even more important as teachers like Halprin and Pauline Koner have a strong theoretical bias which is rather untheatrical. This may perhaps explain why one of their leading pupils, Trisha Brown, has a penchant for works in unusual places, which to date have included a 'dance' across the rooftops of Soho, New York – perhaps more of an event than a performance consisting, as it did, of elaborate semaphore.

Dancers such as James Cunningham, who started study as a drama student in London before working at the Martha Graham School, and Cliff Keuter manage to keep a theatrical element in their works. Keuter trained with Helen Tamiris and Daniel Nagrin and has an obsession with rather unusual props. Cunningham uses the spoken word as part of a mixed-media approach. Remy Charlip is the most theatrical of all and has at various times been a dancer, designer and organizer of children's theater – the Paper Bag Players – and usually a combination of all three. He is one of the great number of people influenced by Merce Cunningham, with whom he danced. Another is Judith Dunn, also a dancer, who is an influential teacher and a choreographer with a dadaesque sense of humor and a cavalier treatment of unsuspecting audiences. Viola Farber, a more intensely serious offshoot of the Cunningham school, creates dances recognizable in the mold of her mentor, dances which are at the same time enigmatic but accessible.

As dance groups come and go there is always the bulk of the iceberg below the surface in colleges and universities keeping alive modern dance. Dances are created and just as soon forgotten. Embalming them in a permanent repertoire is not something most young modern creators want. The event is for the audience and the dancers at that moment. They are both participants; the old idea of the watcher and the watched is being completely broken down. Hundreds of dancers and groups from Toby Armour and her New England Dinosaur to Batya Zamur are in a state of constant creative change. The interchange between modern and classical schools is thriving and the frontiers between the two are slowly being erased. Dance has never been so vital and has never had such a large, involved and deeply committed audience.

Bibliography

There is a wealth of accessible and readable material available, some of which I have relied upon as background reading for this book.

The two dance magazines in Britain, *The Dancing Times* and *Dance and Dancers*, perform different functions. *The Dancing Times*, apart from keeping up to date with current performances has provided very individual coverage of the American scene (including many of the articles which are included in Arlene Croce's excellent book, *After Images*) and an outlet for important historical material, such as Ivor Guest's exciting investigations into Romantic ballet. *Dance and Dancers* gives in-depth coverage to current performances with strong photographic coverage. In America *Dance Magazine* combines the virtues of both, with a very newsy service being performed by *Dance News*.

For dates turn to G.B.L. Wilson's invaluable *Dictionary of Ballet*, now in updated form. No date is entered unquestioned and his exhaustive researches, the result of many trips across Europe, have produced many new facts. Horst Koegler's *Dictionary of Ballet* is similar in format and fills out much detail of dance across Germany and Russia in particular. The large format *Dictionary of Ballet and Modern Dance* by Mary Clarke and David Vaughan includes dates and other relevant facts, but also has many useful background articles on related subjects, ranging from 'Music for Ballet' to 'Ice Dance'.

Modern dance does not have a dictionary as such, but Don MacDonagh has compiled the most informative reference book, which includes not only factual material but also expositions of dances and criticism of a very high standard. Available in paperback, this is an invaluable book, as are the classic writings of American critic Edwin Denby.

A list of other available books for general reading would be immense, but some authors tower above others and must be mentioned. On pre-Romantic ballet Marian Hannah Winter has done masterly research, as has Ivor Guest for the Romantic ballet and its legacy. Richard Buckle has, in *Nijinsky* and *Diaghilev*, brought his critical eye to bear on a period which produced autobiographies of varying degrees of accuracy. His books provide definitive material often confirmed by members of the Diaghilev company still alive.

Photographs of Nijinsky, which show something of his personality, have been collected together in *Nijinsky Dancing*, a large volume with text by Lincoln Kirstein. In much the same manner James Klosty has photographed a genius of our time in his *Merce Cunningham*.

David Vaughan has chronicled the works of Frederick Ashton, and Keith Money has photographed every aspect of the art of Margot Fonteyn. Lavish volumes have been produced to represent the achievements of both American Ballet Theater and The New York City Ballet and if you are a regular ballet-goer, you will have seen the more modest souvenir programs each company produces. Over the years these can form an excellent source of reference and pleasure.

Anneli Alhanko and Per Arthur Segerstrom of the Royal Swedish Ballet rehearsing Macmillan's Romeo and Juliet.

Picture acknowledgments

American Ballet Theater 87, 123, 125; Australian Ballet 1, 31, 48, 65; Myra Armstrong 18; Oscar Bailey 184 bottom; Anthony Crickmay 2, 54, 175; Alan Cunliffe 149; Jesse Davis, Mike Davis Studios 12, 14, 19, 20, 28, 31, 36, 43, 45, 49, 50, 51, 53, 55, 61, 64, 68, 69, 70, 71, 76, 105, 106, 108, 110, 112, 113, 124, 136, 139, 140, 141, 142, 146, 151, 154, 155, 158, 159, 163, 164, 166, 170, 174, 186; Arnold Eagle 91; Johan Elbers 189 top; Christopher Harris 189; Malcolm Hoare 143, 144, 146; James Howell 98; Ingmar Jernberg 30; John R. Johnsen 32, 118; Shuhei Iwamoto 140, 145; Peggy Leder 80, 81, 180, 181, 188; Michel Lidvac 165; Colette Masson 21; National Ballet of Canada 7, 12, 13, 26, 27, 37, 38, 152; Novosti Press Agency 24, 34, 35, 39, 40, 41, 46, 47, 52, 56, 57, 102, 128, 129, 130, 131, 132, 133, 134; Royal Swedish Ballet, Enar Myrkel Rydberg 42, 55, 74, 191; Scottish Ballet 26; Robert Sosenko 187; Leslie Spatt 147, 173; Michael Stannard 115; Martha Swope 90, 93, 178; WNET–13, 92, 92, 106, 118, 119, 172, 176, 177; Jennie Walton 184 top; Rosemary Winckley 182; ZEFA 58, 59, 162, 167, 171.

Index